DREAMS
&
SHADOWS

Dreams & Shadows

First published in 2023 by Witness Books.

Cover design and artwork Neil Williams

979-8-377735168

Introduction…………………………………………………………1

Chapter One: The Novels and Their Place in Traditional Horror
Literature……………………………………………………………6

The Gothic……………………………………………………...8

Folk Horror……………………………………………………14

Cosmic Horror…………………………………………………21

Chapter Two: Atmosphere and Tension: Techniques and Motifs…30

In the Realm of the Senses…………………………………………31

Animal Magic………………………………………………..41

Nightmares and Dreamscapes………………………………………50

Dark Morbidities…………………………………………………56

Moving Experiences………………………………………………...63

There Will Be Blood……………………………………………66

Profondo Rosso…………………………………………………73

Picture This………………………………………………79

The Interconnected World……………………………………82

Chapter Three: The Protagonists……………………………………..86

What's in a Name?..97

Chapter Four: Social Commentary………………………………...107

Chapter Five: Form, Style and Voice………………………………115

Chapter Six: The Nevillesque…………………………………………126

INTRODUCTION

My first encounter with Adam Nevill's writing was when his story *Little Mag's Barrow* appeared in the *Terror Tales of the Lake District* anthology in 2012. I loved the story and found it genuinely scary; it was as if the author had peered into my subconscious, found some images and ideas that disturbed me and put them into a story. Much of what is termed weird fiction sets out to unsettle rather than actually frighten so it was refreshing – and extremely gratifying – to encounter a story that was prepared to aim for the latter of those emotional responses.

It was a story unafraid to use classic horror tropes - an isolated cottage, things literally going bump in the night - but presenting them in such a skilful and atmospheric way that the reader can't help but be drawn in and experience the same fear and emotions as the protagonist.

I now regard it as my gateway drug to his writing: after reading it I immediately purchased two of his novels, *Apartment 16* and *The Ritual* - both of which confirmed my first impressions that here was a writer of supernatural horror to be reckoned with and which further enhanced my appreciation of his skills.

These two novels were actually the second and third written by Adam, his first, *Banquet for the Damned*, was originally published in 2004. A story of supernatural horror set in St Andrews in Scotland, it tells of ancient witch covens and modern day night terrors, and introduced themes and concepts that would feature in many of his subsequent books.

It would be six years (and seventeen drafts) later before his second novel *Apartment 16* was published. Informed by the author's own experiences as a night porter, the horrors this time centre around the activities of Felix Hessen, an artist whose obsession with the "Great Vortex", a portal to another dimension has terrifying implications for the residents of Barrington House, an apartment building in London.

The Ritual was published in 2011 and is probably the best known of the novels by virtue of the film adaptation which was released in 2017. The story concerns a camping and hiking holiday in northern Sweden gone horribly wrong as a group of four friends stumble into an ancient environment where old gods are still worshipped - with violently deadly consequences.

Last Days came next, published a year later in 2012. Set in the world of guerrilla film making, it follows the exploits of Kyle Freeman on his quest to uncover the truth behind a cult, the Temple of the Last Days, rumoured to have participated in occult rituals and whose existence was terminated in a bloody massacre in the Arizona desert.

2013 saw publication of *House of Small Shadows*, with antiques assessor Catherine Howard uncovering much more than she expects during a survey of the contents of the Red House, home of famed taxidermist MH Mason whilst the following year brought us *No One Gets Out Alive*, showcasing an incredibly tense combination of supernatural and psychological horrors as the dark secrets of a rented accommodation in Birmingham, 82 Edgehill Rd, slowly reveal themselves to unwilling tenant Steph.

Lost Girl, which followed in 2015, marked a departure from the supernatural horror of the previous novels, instead offering up a dystopian thriller set in the future in which a father's personal anguish at the kidnapping of his daughter is set against a background of environmental disaster and societal breakdown.

2017's *Under a Watchful Eye* marked a return to the supernatural, a cunningly constructed novel in which a writer becomes embroiled in the activities of a sinister organisation experimenting in astral projection and transmigration.

The Reddening was the first novel to be released through the author's own press Ritual Limited in 2019, the decision to create the press driven by his desire to have more creative control over the books. It's a move that has paid dividends, with the books produced by the company works of art in themselves. Following the publication of two short story collections, *Some Will Not Sleep* and *Hasty For The Dark*, *The Reddening* makes a fine choice of inaugural novel: an epic story of cults, rituals, monsters and sacrifice, of ancient evil and its impact on the present day.

Cunning Folk was the second Ritual Limited novel. Published in 2021 it's an adapted screenplay which is currently still in development, a genesis that is reflected in its use of present tense for the narrative. As the title suggests, folk magic plays a prominent role in the story but, given this is an Adam Nevill novel, the magic is very much of the black variety.

And, most recently, 2022 saw publication of *The Vessel* in which care worker Jess begins a new job at Nerthus House, employed there to look after elderly invalid Flo Gardner, in so doing gradually uncovering the dark history of the house and the horrifying true nature of its owner.

This book is a critique, an exploration of these eleven novels and an examination of the themes and techniques in an attempt to discover what makes these novels so distinctive; what it is about them that appeals so strongly to me and so many other readers: a quest to elucidate the "Nevillesque".

The analysis that follows is by no means an academic one rather it is written in an informal style and in a spirit of admiration and appreciation. Any opinions expressed herein are personal ones. Whilst this investigation will be far from forensic, it is unavoidable that there will be discussion of characters and major plot points and even the endings of some of the novels contained within: here be spoilers. Conversely, some knowledge of the novels prior to reading this is assumed and as such specific characters, plot points will be discussed out of the context provided by the novels. At times I will also use examples from films (as well as literature) to underline points or provide comparisons, something I feel comfortable with given the cinematic nature of Adam's writing.

During the writing of this book I've discovered that I seem to be addicted to footnotes. This is no doubt a reflection of my mind's tendency to frequently wander *off piste* and as such they can often be a distraction from the main text. Suffice to say that reader discretion is advised when confronted by them.

It has been a true labour of love undertaking the re-reads of these novels. There's always a risk that a second voyage through the words will lead to disappointment, a feeling of "that wasn't as good as I remembered" but such was definitely not the case here. Indeed, there were scenes and sequences that I had forgotten about even after such a relatively short time and it was a joy to re-acquaint myself with them. (Sometimes not everything that is read abides). Even taking into account the fact that I was reading the

4

books with a more analytical eye this time, (and stopping frequently to scribble barely legible notes), the experience has only served to enhance my appreciation of them. It's my hope that this book will explain from where that appreciation arises.

Chapter One

The Novels and Their Place in Traditional Horror Literature

The horror genre is a broad church[1], broad enough that it can be divided into sub-categories; just as there is more than one way to skin a cat, there are many ways in which an author can evoke a sense of unease and dread in readers.

Classification is a useful process for readers, enabling them to make an assessment of whether a piece of writing is something they might enjoy – or, conversely, offering an opportunity to try something new[2]. That said, it's rare that any horror novel will fall precisely into one sub-genre alone (although it does happen). Whilst short stories or even novellas are easier to keep within the restraints of a single sub-genre, the length and scope of most novels means that themes and tropes from a variety of sources will be used.

Such is the case with the novels under discussion here. Whilst in some a particular sub-genre will dominate, all of the books display a variety of influences on the writing. In this chapter I'll be looking at how the novels fit into the various sub-genres of horror, highlighting examples from them which demonstrate the criteria for each. This is by

---

[1] Undoubtedly one with a crypt containing ancient tombs and a belltower full of bats.

[2] Categorisation is hugely important in music as well, allowing listeners to select the type of music which they enjoy and which literally strikes a chord with them. Trying different things is fine too of course, and the categorisation of musical styles allows an informed choice to be made. If there were no labels, and choices were made blind, the nightmare scenario of buying an album because it looks interesting only to discover upon playing that it's jazz would be too horrible to contemplate.

no means a comprehensive list and there are undoubtedly examples I will have missed. Conversely, there is also the distinct possibility that I will occasionally wander off-topic and that I end up including themes that don't fit perfectly into the genre being discussed.

There is of course much discussion as to what defines one particular sub-genre and what makes it different to others. My approach here is to use fairly broad brush strokes in terms of identifying their various characteristics. My definition of traditional is also open to discussion; devotees of Splatterpunk may be violently aggrieved at its omission (although blood *will* be spilt later on in the book), similarly aficionados of body horror may feel bereft[3] but a line has to be drawn somewhere and the three categories which follow have been chosen as they best encompass the horrors found within these novels.

"Traditional" of course implies a degree of antiquity, a long history and being well established. Surprisingly, the term "folk horror" wasn't coined until the 1970s (at least in terms of a descriptor for horror films) but the type of horror it describes has been around for a lot longer than that and is possibly the oldest of the sub-genres discussed here, firmly rooted as it is in folkloric traditions that date back centuries.

The term Cosmic Horror arises from the work of H P Lovecraft, the originator of the literary philosophy of Cosmicism although some of the concepts associated with it have been an integral part of the horror genre from long before he began writing. Given its base concept of the insignificance of human existence, it's a kind of irony that the genre it spawned has gained such a significant place in the world of horror fiction and has become as much a

---

[3] Or have a chip on their shoulder, or an ear, or possibly a mouth.

traditional part of horror literature as the gothic – the genre with which this discussion begins.

The Gothic

The literary term "gothic" is a direct reference to the architectural style of the middle ages. Buildings constructed in this style provided the locations used in the earliest examples of the genre, most notably in what is regarded as the first gothic novel, *The Castle of Otranto* by Horace Walpole, published in 1764[4].

This particular component of the gothic aesthetic was employed in a hugely effective way in Adam's first novel *Banquet For the Damned*. The story is set in the ancient town of St Andrews in Scotland, a place dominated by the ruins of its medieval cathedral which stand on the eastern edge of the town, perched above the crashing waves of the North Sea. Anyone who has visited cannot fail to be impressed by the sight, to feel the sense of awe that ancient buildings evoke. Beth, a major player in the novel, at one point remarks:

"A ruin has its own magic. Old, forgotten things do."

A sentiment which perfectly encapsulates the gothic ethos, as well as the feel of the novel itself which uses its setting impeccably to evoke a sense of lingering dread and unease. It's not just the cathedral that lends atmosphere, it's the whole town with its narrow, twisting alleyways and ancient buildings – the university in which some of the action is set was established in the fifteenth century

---

[4] The second edition was subtitled "A Gothic Story" just to emphasise the point.

and is the oldest in Scotland (and the third oldest English speaking university in the world).

Whilst the narrative of *Banquet For the Damned* unfolds over a number of locations, that of *House of Small Shadows* is limited to a single location; a building which fits nicely into the gothic template. The Red House stands in glorious isolation, separated from the nearest village by woods and surrounded by a high wall covered in ivy with a black gate granting access to the grounds. On her first viewing of it, the book's protagonist, Catherine,

> *...felt nostalgic for a time she wasn't even sure was part of her own experience, and Imagined she was passing into another age.*

The Red House is certainly old, a prerequisite for any gothic location, not quite a stately home but large enough to incorporate wings and with windows giving the impression of eyes gazing out at the landscape around it. Finials and iron spikes adorn the roof like hackles rising on a dog's back. The lane which approaches the house is described as being there a long time before the building was[5] and passes through a natural tunnel formed by overhanging trees.

Whilst the house itself is gothic enough, what lurks inside is even more so. Displays of anthropomorphic taxidermy fill the Red House, creations of its previous resident M H Mason. Whilst the dioramas are in themselves distinctly unsettling, their presence creates the impression that the house is somehow frozen in Victorian times, when such adornments were seen as *de rigueur*,

---

[5] Both times I read the book I wondered if this might be a hint that the Red House is built on a ley-line, Alfred Watkins' Old Straight Track.

highlighting another feature of the gothic: the past intruding upon the present.

This Victorian aesthetic is further enhanced by the house's occupant, Mason's niece Edith. Ninety three years old and wheelchair-bound, with a powdered wig in a style not fashionable since the early nineteen-hundreds she is the archetypal Victorian lady of the house (complete with a mute housemaid). It's impossible not to draw comparisons with Dickens' Miss Havisham, described by the author himself in *Great Expectations* as "the witch of the place". Although younger than Edith, her self-imposed confinement in Satis House has aged her prematurely. Both women are bound to the gothic buildings in which they live as a result of tragedy – Miss Havisham jilted and defrauded on her wedding day, Edith Mason devastated by the suicide of her uncle.

The apartment buildings in *Apartment 16* and *No One Gets Out Alive,* despite being polar opposites in terms of luxury and comfort, both offer up further examples of gothic dwellings to be found in Adam's novels. Both are examples of Victorian builds with, as it turns out, dark and unpleasant histories which again directly affect the current residents; the past once more impacting on the present.

Nerthus House, the residence of Flo Gardner in *The Vessel*, is another fine example of a gothic location. Situated in the village of Eadric, the former vicarage is centrally located within the village, and its position as the hub of a wheel surrounded by the spokes of other buildings is a deeply significant one in the context of the novel, fitting into the motif of circularity which runs through the narrative. An ominous description of the house is given by one of the neighbours:

"Nerthus House remains under a shadow. Even on a day as beautiful as this..."

The same neighbour later passes comment on Flo herself, telling Jess that:

"...the past is always with her."

Which is about as gothic a description of a character as you can get.

The classic gothic image of an isolated and derelict house is best conjured up by Hunter's Tor, the remote cottage on Dartmoor which is the setting for the finale of *Under A Watchful Eye*. The location of M L Hazzard's Society of Psychophysical Research[6], its mystique enhanced by it appearing as a blurred image on Google Earth, some dark feature of the building itself making it "immune" to modern technology.

The house provides the setting for one of Adam's most effective sequences in which the book's protagonist Seb spends a night there, only to be visited by an array of ghostly apparitions. Ghosts, and the haunted houses in which they dwell, are another traditional staple of the gothic and they've made appearances in a number of the Nevill novels.

In *Apartment 16*, the revenants don't appear in the titular building, rather in the seedy digs of joint protagonist Seth above the Green Man pub. A frequent visitor to his room is the ghost of a young, abused girl but at one point late on in the book, a look outside reveals a

---

[6] A pseudo-scientific organisation. Mixing science and the gothic seems almost oxymoronic but of course there is a fine history of the two coming together (*Frankenstein, The Strange Case of Dr Jekyll & Mr Hyde* and so many others). In a genre that embraces the uncanny, a search for explanations will always have a place.

host of deceased former tenants. There is, of course, an element of ambiguity to these appearances as over the course of the novel Seth's mental faculties are gradually eroded as the malevolent forces present in the apartment building in which he works begin to take control of him.

It could be argued too that the apparitions Seb encounters at Hunter's Tor aren't "real" ghosts. Hazzard's research involved experimentation with translocation and astral projection; the uncoupling of body and soul. The suggestion is that the spectres Seb sees are the results of successful experiments, the disembodied souls of the members of the Society rather than the remnants of the deceased, forever doomed to haunt the place where they died[7].

The only ghosts which are undoubtedly "real" appear to great effect in *No One Gets Out Alive*. (Thereby making 82 Edgehill Rd a genuine haunted house). They are the spirits of all the girls who have been murdered in the house prior to protagonist Steph's arrival and make their appearances in a number of traditional ways; whispered voices, a drop in temperature, the sound of crying and as a tangible presence within Steph's room. There's even a full form apparition at one point, an introduction cleverly handled by the author as it's only until events have come to a head that it's revealed that the figure seen in the garden is actually a ghost.

The spirits presented here are benign manifestations, seeking out Steph's help rather than trying to harm her. It's a nice counterpoint to the actions and behaviour of landlord Knacker McGuire – a man who starts out "helping" Steph from the predicament she finds herself in

---

[7] Which is about as academic an argument as you can get really. (But could give rise to a new variation of the internet meme: "It's only a ghost if it's from the ghost region of France, otherwise it's just sparkling apparition").

but who ends up as a deadly threat to her. In effect, Steph is imprisoned in 82 Edgehill Rd by Knacker (and his cousin Fergal) a scenario which is another trope of gothic fiction. An early incarnation of this was in Ann Radcliffe's 1794 novel *The Mysteries of Udolpho* in which the dastardly villain Montoni imprisons the novel's heroine Emily St Aubert in the gloomy, ancient eponymous castle and is one which has appeared numerous times in the gothic since.

In *House of Small Shadows*, Catherine faces a similar situation and finds herself unable to escape from the clutches of the Red House. Partly this is due to her own character, diminished and weakened by the hardships of life[8] but later by proactive efforts from Edith and her mysterious maid Maude who even drug her at one point to ensure compliance.

The classic dynamic of imprisonment in gothic novels is that of a female victim and male perpetrator. That dynamic is partly turned on its head in *The Ritual*, in which protagonist Luke finds himself the prisoner. Whilst the members of Blood Frenzy, the Black Metal group who are his captors, are about as far removed from the archetypal sophistication of the gothic villain, their efforts still manage to create the psychological horror which is so much a part of the imprisonment scenario. This horror arises as much from the unstable nature of the captors as the depravations resulting from the confinement itself, and a similar scenario is present in *The Reddening*, with Katrine, one of the novel's twin protagonists, held against her will by the cult members she dubs "Beard" and "Headscarf".

Whilst the imprisonments of classic gothic literature are usually a means to some twisted, romantic end, those

---

[8] A characteristic she shares with innumerable gothic heroines.

described in Adam's novels are for much darker reasons – the procurement of victims for sacrificial purposes, a trope much used in the next sub-genre to be discussed.

Folk Horror

The act of sacrifice, specifically the killing of animals or humans[9], is an act of worship, more often than not a form of propitiation; appeasing and/or pleasing a deity in exchange for some kind of favour (or the avoidance of retribution). This favour is often a guarantee of fertility for farmland, a promise of bountiful harvests, that guarantee possible because of the link between the deities and the land in which they dwell and the power they have over it. As a character in The Reddening puts it:

"They goes in the red and we is gifted."

Sacrifice is a staple of the folk horror genre, the horror arising both from the nature of the killing itself, often prolonged and painful to cause as much suffering as possible, but also from those carrying out the rituals and ceremonies; the true believers who see the act as celebratory - cultists immune to the dreadfulness, not to mention the illegality, of taking another's life.

Such sacrifices are usually the culmination of a ritual, a prescribed set of actions which provides the title of Adam's third novel. *The Ritual* does indeed feature a rite of sacrifice but one which – slightly ironically – comes to nothing, sabotaged as it is by the old woman whose house provides the location of protagonist Luke's confinement in the second half of the novel. (Although the film version

---

[9] Humans are animals of course. Some more than others.

does feature a successful one). The sabotage is committed not out of any pity or concern for Luke, rather as a way of dealing with those she deems unworthy to uphold the ancient traditions of worship for the forest's "original occupant[10]".

Those unworthy individuals are "Blood Frenzy", a black metal band who have appropriated the mythology as part of their shtick, trivialising the "old ways" and effectively disrespecting tradition. They are described in the book as

...vandals; impatient, delinquent, angry.

and provide some (albeit bleak and dark) comic relief as a result of their ineptitude and misplaced self-aggrandisement.

This misappropriation of ancient traditions is also a feature of *The Reddening*. The worship of this book's ancient god dates back to prehistoric times, as evidenced by the archaeological details which are described in the opening chapters. The horrors associated with it have been rekindled however, both as a result of quarrying activity in the region and also the arrival of musician Tony Willows and his entourage who – much like Blood Frenzy in *The Ritual* – align themselves with the mythology, resurrecting and re-establishing the ancient rites of worship and sacrifice.

Whereas Blood Frenzy's impertinence at dabbling in things where they shouldn't results in their plans being thwarted, such is not the case here and the inevitable outcome of unleashing forces beyond one's control –

---

[10] The Original Occupant is the title of one of Adam's short stories, a precursor to the novel set in the same region of northern Scandinavia.

15

things getting horribly, and horrifically out of hand – is exactly what happens.

(The sacrifice scene in *The Reddening* is one of the outstanding set-pieces of Adam's novels. Shocking and disturbing, it will be discussed in greater detail later on in the book).

The trope of meddling in things and losing control is a well-established one in horror fiction of course. *Frankenstein; or the Modern Prometheus* is an iconic example and there are the many Lovecraftian protagonists who summon Old Ones only to regret it later – *The Dunwich Horror* a specific instance of this scenario. It's also seen in Adam's first novel, *Banquet For The Damned*, in which an ancient coven of witches (ironically resurrected by scientific research) wreak havoc in present day St Andrews[11].

The act of sacrifice is also to be found in *No One Gets Out Alive*, the residents of 82 Edgehill Rd – after having been exploited by the owners – eventually end up as sacrificial victims for the entity known as Black Maggie with death by garrotting their ultimate fate. The original reason for the sacrifices was propitiation, lives were offered up by way of a bargain with Black Maggie in return for guaranteed fertility of the land. Despite the fact that that land now lies within the environs of the city of Birmingham, the ritual continues, suggesting a shift from the bargaining nature of the original sacrifices to a more

---

[11] See also the election of Boris Johnson to the leadership of the Conservative Party, a classic example of knowingly unleashing a malevolent force and then coming to regret the consequences. And then, in a perfect example of life imitating art, to be succeeded by Liz Truss – much as *The Bride of Frankenstein* was a sequel to James Whales' original film. That film ends with the classic line "we belong dead!" of course, a phrase definitely worthy of consideration as a new party motto.

appeasing role; Black Maggie must now be kept happy for fear of unleashing terrible revenge.

Ritual murder has a big part to play in *The Vessel* too. The title of the novel is a clever one which can be taken to mean a variety of things but one interpretation is a literal one: a reference to the wicker cage in which the sacrificial victims are drowned after having suffered ritual dismemberment.

As mentioned in the opening chapter of this section, ritualistic sacrifice often involves animals as well as humans[12]. Prior to the sacrifice of Steve in *The Reddening*, an unfortunate pony suffers the same fate and in *Cunning Folk*, the Moots, aka the neighbours from hell, are responsible for the deaths of numerous woodland critters, all by way of appeasement to the old god which dwells in the earth beside them: The Sow Beneath the Earth.

The Moots are the titular cunning folk – an arcane term for folk healers and/or practitioners of magic. The magic performed by the cunning folk was of a benign type, used for the benefit of their fellow men and women but the Moots present a much darker version of this, are in actuality devotees of harm-orientated witchcraft with curses a speciality.

Witches and witchcraft are a core constituent of the folklore of many countries and as a result often feature in tales of folk horror, traditional and otherwise. *Cunning Folk* has a witch and warlock as its antagonists and in *The Vessel*, there's very strong evidence that Flo Gardener and the other female residents of Eadric are members of a coven – Flo uses "merry meet" and "merry part" rather

---

[12] Everyone remembers Edward Woodward trapped inside the Wicker Man but there were goats in there too. (None of them making any attempt to kick through the flimsy structure in order to escape it has to be said).

than "hello" and "goodbye", terminology used by devotees of Wicca and intones the name of the Celtic goddess Erce,[13]

Witchcraft plays a major part in *Banquet For The Damned* too. As mentioned earlier, the horrors that are unleashed into the present day take the form of an ancient coven of witches, summoned from the past to attack those responsible by unleashing a familiar, the terrifying Brown Man who hunts down his victims via night terrors which become terrifying reality. The rituals for summoning the Brown Man involve dressing in animal skins, the participants then actually taking on the form of the animals themselves - something that's mentioned in passing in *Banquet For The Damned* but which assumes prominence in *Cunning Folk*, alongside another well-established feature of witchcraft, backwards dancing. There's possession here too, Beth, a major player in the novel, is taken over by the spirit of one of the witches, in order to facilitate their return[14].

The members of The Kings, the cult that feature in *Lost Girl* are described as shamans and that's an appellation given to Henry Strader, the first "Martyr of Rod and String", who provides the dark backstory for *House of Small Shadows*, a shaman who transmitted the thoughts of ancient gods via the medium of puppetry. His martyrdom was a result of his being tried and found guilty of sedition and witchcraft, leading to his execution by being "broken upon the wheel", a particularly gruesome form of torture in which bones are broken by an

---

[13] It's no coincidence that the events of *Cunning Folk* unfold just outside of Eadric.

[14] Via a proposed ritual sacrifice of the novels' protagonist Dante no less…

iron bar, before an angry mob descended upon him to dismember his remains[15].

A martyr is someone who sacrifices themselves in defence of a religious belief and religion plays a huge role in folk horror. It's often the case that the god in question doesn't actually appear in the story, the horror instead arising from the worshippers themselves, their mindless devotion driving them to commit atrocities in the name of whichever deity they are in thrall to.

It's the secretive nature of these cults that also generates horror; a classic folk horror trope is the arrival of an outsider, usually in a remote rural location, who is mystified by the strange behaviour of the locals before gradually uncovering the dark secrets they are keeping.

That premise is used to the full in *The Reddening*, with outsider Helene stumbling into unimaginable horror as she tries to uncover information about her brother. The cult she uncovers are the Red People, so named because their bodies are covered in red dye, whose belief system drives them to kill, not only for sacrificial ritual but also to protect the secrets they keep from the outside world. Their first appearance in the book is truly chilling, a vignette in which they encircle a pair of campers on a beach, that circle growing ever tighter as the attack begins.

Whilst Helene stumbles unwittingly into the activities of the Red People, the protagonist of *Last Days*, Kyle Freeman, proactively enters the world of a cult – the Temple of the Last Days. Indeed, his investigation into the cult and its activities provides the narrative thrust of the novel.

---

[15] An activity that will find echoes in the sacrifice scene in *The Reddening*.

In a departure from standard folk horror cult behaviour, the Temple of the Last Days do not worship a specific deity, rather they are on a mission to bring about a ritual known as the Ascent in which they will leave behind the restrictions of their mortal existence and rise to a higher plane of being.

The cult is led by the charismatic Sister Katherine and bears close resemblance to the Manson Family, its members forced to eke out an ascetic lifestyle whilst its leader resides in the lap of luxury.

Whilst the residents of the apartment building featured in *Apartment 16* certainly act together in a common cause, it's probably stretching things to call them a cult[16] however, a stronger case could be made for the residents of Hunter's Tor in *Under a Watchful Eye*, members of M L Hazzard's Society of Psychophysical Research who allow themselves to be experimented on to test his theories of astral projection and translocation – whilst paying significant sums of money for the privilege.

The aforementioned Kings are a cult whose activities, alongside the global environmental apocalypse, provide a backdrop to the story of *Lost Girl*. Given the dystopia the world has become, the cult has become a gang, a crime syndicate in charge of neighbourhoods through which the novel's protagonist searches for his kidnapped daughter.

King Death is the personification of the deity they worship, a robed and skeletal figure whose image is graffitied on walls and buildings but it's the process of death itself which is the cult's obsession: the transition from one state of being to another. In what is probably the least overtly horrific of Adam's novels (in a supernatural

---

[16] This is definitely the case in Adam's short story To Forget and Be Forgotten however, which also features a group of elderly residents in a London apartment building who perform some very strange rituals indeed.

sense at least), the sections featuring the Kings provide a welcome frisson of unease and disquiet.

The Kings provide a departure from the classic folk horror ideal of a cult in that they are based in urban areas. As stated earlier, a rural location is usually the norm, preferably somewhere remote and isolated in order to allow the adherents to practice their faith and rituals without disturbances from the outside world.

With the exception of *Apartment 16* and *Lost Girl*, all of the novels featuring a folk horror influence make use of rural locations, most notably the isolated Red House of *House of Small Shadows*, the ancient forests of northern Scandinavia in *The Ritual* and the south coast region of the UK which is the setting for *The Reddening*. As is the case in most categorisations, there is some degree of overlap between defining components and the setting of a story, the landscape in which the action takes place, is just as much a feature of the next sub-genre to be examined.

Cosmic Horror

Cosmic dread arises when an individual is confronted by something so beyond their comprehension that the only response to it as a mixture of fear and awe. To be reminded of one's own insignificance in the grand scheme of things is an unsettling experience.[17]

Finding oneself in a dramatic landscape can have such an effect. Whilst appreciating the beauty on display, part of your emotional response (albeit on a subliminal, subconscious level) is to be a little bit afraid. It's a phenomenon I've experienced many times and one which I realised was not mine alone when, as part of an English class at secondary school, we studied *The Prelude* by

---

[17] But one I recommend.

William Wordsworth. In it, he describes a night-time boat trip in the Lake District thus:

And, as I rose upon the stroke, my boat went heaving
through the water like a swan.
When, from behind that craggy steep till then the
horizon's bound, a huge peak, black and huge, as if with
voluntary power instinct, upreared its head.
I struck and struck again, and growing still in stature the
grim shape towered up between me and the stars, and
still, for so it seemed, with purpose of its own and,
measured motion like a living thing, strode after me.
With trembling oars I turned, and through the silent water
stole my way back to the covert of the willow tree.

What Wordsworth is describing here is classic cosmic awe and dread and it's a concept also expressed by Algernon Blackwood in his story *The Willows*:

Mountains overawe and oceans terrify, while the mystery
of great forests exercises a spell peculiarly its own.

This feeling of insignificance in the face of natural wonder is echoed by a number of characters in Adam's novels. In *Banquet For The Damned*, Eliot Coldwell describes standing on a pier next to rough seas during a storm as:

"I felt close to something powerful."

And later on in the book expresses the opinion:

"What do we know about our place amongst the stars?
We're blind to anything beyond the material."

In *The Reddening*, Shelley – one of the campers to fall victim to the Red People in the book's opening chapters – feels that same insignificance, a feeling shared later on in the book by Helene as she retraces her brother's steps across the landscape:

> *Being in the presence of open sea… conjures a sense of deep personal insignificance and an acute vulnerability before an insurmountable, barely known presence.*

Proximity to the sea brings about a similar reaction in Seb, protagonist of *Under A Watchful Eye*:

> *Exposed to the vast sky and the expanse of the sea, the great spaces enlarged Seb's fear until he doubted he'd ever felt as insignificant.*

The fear elicited by the power of nature is not irrational. Earthquakes, tsunamis, wildfires, volcanic eruptions and hurricanes are just some of the ways that power can be unleashed to devastating effect. In the section on folk horror, the concept of mankind meddling with things they shouldn't, ultimately unleashing a horror they can't control was discussed - which serves as a frighteningly accurate description of the climate crisis that provides the backdrop to *Lost Girl*.

This is perhaps the most overtly cosmic horror to feature in all of Adam's books; the planet itself is taking revenge on mankind, a force beyond comprehension is ridding itself of an irritating problem – humans truly are insignificant in the face of such power[18].

---

[18] This idea of global warming as cosmic horror is given even more prominence in Adam's short story *Call the Name* in which environmental catastrophe is linked directly to the Cthulhu mythos.

Part of the awe and dread associated with landscapes arises simply from their age. The lifespans of humans are no more than a blink of an eye when compared to the geography and geology of the world in which they live. It was there a long time before mankind appeared and will be there long after their departure.

Much is made of the ancient nature of the forest in which Luke and his hiking companions get lost in *The Ritual*. It is described as the oldest forest in Europe and is undoubtedly a character itself within the book, seemingly possessed of a malevolent spirit and actively working against the hikers, keeping them trapped within its dark embrace. The descriptions of the forest are wonderful, conveying perfectly the claustrophobia and oppression created by the density of trees, piling on the tension as the friends get more and more disorientated and lost[19].

This ancient aspect of the landscape is also a feature of *The Reddening*. There's great emphasis in the book's opening chapters on the prehistory of the area and the uncovered evidence of the cannibalistic rituals that occurred then, and which continue to the present day. The longevity of the deities being worshipped in both of these examples suggests an immortal aspect to them – what hope does mankind have against a threat which cannot be killed?

The area – a fictionalised composite of real and actual locations - in which *The Reddening* is set is coastal, a liminal space, a border if you will. The same applies to St Andrews in *Banquet For The Damned*. Borders have long had the reputation of being magical places and are frequently chosen as locations for horror stories, a trend

---

[19] Something that was captured brilliantly in the film adaptation of the novel. A special shout out must go to the location coordinator, the forest they chose to film in was perfect and the cinematography to make the trees like the bars of a cage outstanding.

that features in some of Adam's novels too. The forest in *The Ritual* straddles the border between Norway and Sweden, the Red House of *House of Small Shadows* sits on the border of England and Wales and the location of the Temple of the Last Days' bloody endgame is the Sonoran Desert of Arizona on the border with Mexico.

The choice of physical borders as locations adds a subliminal context to the stories, tapping into the notion that these are the places of magic mentioned above. Metaphysical borders – or references to them - are also scattered throughout the novels.

The presence of other planes of existence overlapping with our own is postulated by Hart Miller in *Banquet For The Damned*:

> *"...another place, governed by different laws. Called by different names… and then forgotten until someone created a gap where the walls are thinnest between that place and this[20]."*

It's a belief shared by M L Hazzard in *Under A Watchful Eye*, who theorises that Hades, Paradise and the real world overlap, "interpenetrate" each other and that:

> *"… the inhabitants of [each realm] are never far away from us… discarnate soul-bodies are all around us… the incarnate and discarnate are all overlapping, all of the time, in different spheres that exist simultaneously in the same place, but don't interact."*

In *Apartment 16*, one of the gaps mentioned by Miller is actually opened by the artist Felix Hessen, thereby creating the Great Vortex and allowing the infiltration of,

---

[20] Possibly when "the stars are right"

and access to, another dimension. The novel makes great use of mirrors and reflected images, something that enhances the theme of different realities looking in on one another.

The border between life and death is the focus of The Kings in *Lost Girl* whose whole belief system is predicated on the transition from life to death, the latter not an end to things but a new beginning, a different kind of existence. As Oleg, a member of the Kings who plays an important role in the novel, death is:

"not terminus, but transitus"

The "Afterdeath" of the Kings is populated by "patrons", guardian angels who assist new arrivals. It's a concept that also appears in *Under A Watchful Eye*, although the "Hinderers" that dwell in this version of the afterlife have a less benign outlook on life[21] whilst the Ritual of Ascent, the ultimate goal of Sister Katherine and her followers in *Last Days*, is an attempt to cross the border into another plane of existence, to transcend death itself, the border that the terrifying Blood Friends cross back and forth over as they hunt down their prey.

Sometimes the characters in the novels actually manage to cross these metaphysical borders. Both *Cunning Folk* and *The Reddening* feature underground chambers, or lairs, the dwelling places of their respective deities which are discovered by the books' protagonists. The size and layout of these chambers give the impression that they cannot exist within the geography of the real world around and above them, suggesting that they are overlapping realities, only accessible to the chosen few.

---

[21] Or, technically, death.

The hallucinatory visions experienced by those interlopers only serve to emphasise this impression.

The inhabitants of these chambers may be gods to some but to most are simply monsters. Strange and unnatural, their mere appearance enough to instil fear and dread in the observer, it is their unknowability that makes them so frightening, their power and rage. It is their links with the landscape in which they dwell and their indifference towards humanity that makes their horror cosmic.

As someone who appreciates a good monster, I find it most gratifying that Adam embraces the concept of them wholeheartedly; where others might shy away from such a traditional way to instil fear he has instead gone on to create some truly terrifying creatures with which to populate his novels.

Moder, the creature that haunts the Scandinavian forest of *The Ritual*, differs from the other Nevill monsters in that she roams freely throughout her environment, is not confined to a lair and kept in check. Although present throughout the novel, it is not until the final pages that she makes a real entrance, doing so in a frantic chase scene which allows only glimpses of her overall form, presenting a series of images and impressions to create the picture of what she actually looks like to the reader:

A thick-haired face, black with a wet, bovine muzzle...
mostly goatish... the greatest of horns...

A similar approach is taken with regards to Old Creel, the monster worshipped by the Red People in *The Reddening*. Whereas Moder's ancestry (assuming she is "young" enough to have one) is ungulate in nature, cervid or caprine[22], Creel's is definitely canine. This knowledge is obtained not through detailed descriptions of the monster – because there aren't any – but from hints and clues seeded throughout the book which point towards the nature of the beast. It's a classic example of less is more; eschewing detailed description allows readers to create their own images, engaging their imagination in the way all good writing should.

The chthonic deity in the follow up novel *Cunning Folk* is also bereft of any detailed description. Indeed, when protagonist Tom finally confronts it, its face is hidden behind a cowl. Scant it may be, but what description there is is enough to conjure up a terrifying image of this porcine beast, with its black, hirsute legs terminating in trotters extending from beneath its robes[23].

A well-established trope in cosmic horror is that when these monsters are encountered, when the appalling truth is uncovered, the experience is so overwhelming that the protagonists are unable to cope with it, descending into madness and insanity as a result.

With regards to Adam's novels, this template is followed most closely in *The Reddening*, in which Kat ends up committed to a psychiatric hospital after her experiences with Old Creel and the Red People. A similar fate is experienced by Tom, in *Cunning Folk* and the unnamed father in *Lost Girl* although it's more the case that it's the relentless pressure they find themselves under through the course of the novels that brings about the disintegration of their characters rather than specific exposure to a monstrous entity.

---

[22] Think Black Phillip on steroids. (Or Black Phillipa in this case).

[23] To say nothing of the amazing artwork which graces the cover of the book.

It's in *The Ritual* however that the most dramatic – and therefore the most typically cosmic – destruction of a character's body and soul is found. By the end of the novel, Luke – the only survivor of the hiking party which ventures into the ancient forest – is completely broken; forced to kill to survive. Come the story's conclusion he is literally naked, bloody and bruised, described as:

... fear and white eyes inside a suit of dirty skin

Despite escaping the clutches of Moder, the horrors he has witnessed, and been forced into committing himself, have changed him forever. He may have survived – but at what cost? Moder, of course, survives too. Frustrated perhaps, irritated by the trespassers in her domain, but ultimately indifferent to Luke and what may become of him in the future. She persists, (an achievement she shares with all the Nevill supernatural foes come the end of the novels), and therein lies the real horror.

Chapter Two

Creating Atmosphere and Tension: Techniques and Motifs

The appreciation of art is entirely personal. What one person regards as the epitome of creative endeavour may well elicit a *meh* from someone else. No amount of discussion between them will change the mind of either participant; a piece of art either connects with you emotionally or it doesn't.[24]

The reasons as to why a particular artist should appeal to an individual, may even become their favourite, is beyond the scope of this book[25]but must surely involve a connection between the observer and elements within the art itself. Something about the style of a piece of art speaks to the viewer/listener/reader. If an artist reuses these stylistic elements in subsequent creations then that appreciation is reinforced.

Whilst a negative interpretation of this recurring use of techniques and stylistic choices is that it shows a lack of originality, or even creativity, a more positive outlook (and one I share) is that it is evidence of true and consistent artistic voice.

Indeed, within the world of cinema, those directors whose consistency of tone and style are regarded as auteurs. Films are of course a visual medium and a number of directors will make use of the same technique(s) and images whilst presenting their stories.

Examples include the so-called "Kubrick Stare", in which actors tilt their head slightly forward and stare at

---

[24] Some people like jazz..

[25] And my expertise.

the camera from beneath lowered brows. The pose has featured in most of his films and is iconic enough to bear his name (and is now regarded as "the" way to suggest incipient madness and/or scheming in all films).

Wes Anderson's films are immediately identifiable by the precise symmetry of his shots, with characters invariably situated directly in the centre of the frame, whilst a film in which the film stock changes multiple times throughout its running time will probably have been directed by Oliver Stone. Alfonso Cuarón makes repeated use of long takes, a technique also employed by Sam Mendes and Steve McQueen – the latter tending to keep the camera fixed rather than tracking the action, lending an intensity (which is sometimes unbearable) to the scenes being filmed.

These various techniques can be regarded as characteristic of the directors involved, their signature moves so to speak, and the same can be said of the motifs and techniques employed by Adam when constructing his novels. Whilst his style and form provide the content of a later chapter, what now follows is a discussion of those specific instances which can define a book as "Nevillesque".

In the Realm of the Senses

Depending on which reference sources you wish to believe, the phrase "things that go bump in the night" is derived from an ancient litany of either Scottish or Cornish origin. The prayer beseeches protection specifically from "ghoulies and ghosties, and long-legged beasties" as well as the more generic bumping things themselves. Which are, of course, the scariest of all the threats listed; at least with the ghouls, ghosts and leggy beasts the threat is a known one. An unexpected sound (particularly one heard in the dark) provokes an immediate fear response, sparking the imagination into coming up with the most pessimistic and terrifying explanations for what has caused it. Which, in horror stories, generally turn out to be correct.

The use of sound effects in horror films is widespread but it's also a technique which can be used in literature to create tension. Films have it easier of course, being able to produce the sound/s so that viewers can experience them directly. Making use of sound in writing requires more work, the sounds have to be described in such a way that their presence in the narrative elicits the same emotional responses but that's a challenge Adam has risen to and his novels are littered with prime examples of aural terror.

Two of the novels have prologues in which sounds play a major role. In *Apartment 16*, nightwatchman Seth hears an array of sounds coming from behind the locked door of the titular, unoccupied, apartment; the clatter of furniture on a marble floor, something heavy being dragged across it, a door opening inside and then the sound of voices – cries, moans and screams.

It's a hugely effective opening to the book, setting the scene and telegraphing much of what is to follow. Similarly, in *Last Days*, a sound-laden prologue introduces (at least the concept of) the Blood Friends, the monstrous entities which are hunting down the surviving members of the Temple of the Last Days as a woman returns to her home in Denver to hear the *bump-bump-bump* of the creatures moving around in her rented apartment.

Whilst the sounds Seth hears are projections – there is nothing physically inside the room to make them – the Blood Friends are very much flesh and blood and the use of sound as an indicator of physical presence is a common feature of Adam's novels.

The scuttling and scrabbling of something awful moving across a wall first appears in the night terror experienced by Maria in *Banquet For The Damned* and also features in the shared dream experience of Seb and Becky in *Under A Watchful Eye*. The remote cottage which is a key location of *Banquet For The Damned* offers up more "something bad is in there" sound effects with loud banging from within greeting the arrival of academics Henry and Arthur and, later when protagonist Dante arrives, as he hears the movements of the man he has come to find in an upstairs room, the crying which accompanies these sounds serves to increase the tension of the scene, that tension mounting even further as Dante begins to climb the stairs…

When Tom and his family move into their new home in *Cunning Folk*, his first experiences with his neighbours the Moots come via sound: from over the fence come the *snip* of secateurs and a (nicely character-defining) sigh at the exuberance of Tom's daughter Gracey. Noisy banging, heard through the walls of the house precede their first actual sighting.

Perhaps the most effective use of sounds indicating an unseen presence come in *The Ritual*. Throughout the first half of the book Luke and his friends are stalked by Moder and for much of that time the creature remains hidden from view. It's the sound of breaking branches as Moder moves through the forest and then the barks, yips and bestial grunts of the creature that give away her presence, instilling fear in the hikers and readers alike. Moder's attacks generally happen off screen but one – the abduction of Hutch – is described, employing masterful use of sound rather than imagery; from within his own tent Luke hears the attack, the ripping of cloth and the screams of his friend.[26]

This implication of violence and horror through sound is also used effectively in *The Reddening*. Prior to his own sacrifice, Steve has to listen to the same ordeal being experienced by a pony, creating a horrific anticipation of what is to come for both himself and the reader and, later on in the book, Helene hears rather than sees the destruction generated by Old Creel's rampage.

As well as being indicators of activity and presence, the sounds themselves are capable of delivering chills. Already mentioned are the yips, barks and grunts of Moder suggesting the bestial nature of the as yet unseen creature. The barking of dogs is certainly a sound which can instil fear[27], even in real life and makes an appearance in some of Adam's novels. Other than *The Reddening*, with its canine-centric horrors both natural and supernatural, the barking of dogs is a sound frequently heard emanating from the Arizona compound of Sister Katherine and her followers in *Last Days*. The animals run freely around the compound but the most significant occurrence of their barking is heard on the night when the cult meets its bloody demise, the clamour a result not just

---

[26] Which is how the scene plays out in the film. Kudos again to the makers of the movie adaptation for the sound design. Even the opening titles are overlaid with disconcerting sounds rather than music and the "hear not see" approach of the book with regards to Moder's stalking is recreated brilliantly.

[27] Something William Friedkin was very aware of when making The Exorcist. The cut to the fighting dogs in the scene where Father Merrin first encounters the statue of Pazuzu acts almost like a jump scare and barking is later incorporated into the soundtrack – a subliminal aural cue to go with the visual ones in the film.

of the slaughter around them but their own involvement in the final rite performed by the cult[28].

During Seb's first encounter with Thin Len, the terrifying apparition who haunts the pages of *Under A Watchful Eye*, he hears a voice which degrades into "something canine." The transition from human to canine is scary enough but simply hearing the voice in the first place brings its own terrors. Whilst the sound of barking, or any of the other animal noises that occur throughout Adam's books, invoke real fear, it's more a sense of unease and dread – melancholy even - that a disembodied voice brings with it.

As well as the voices heard in the aforementioned *Under A Watchful Eye* and *Apartment 16*, there are others to be experienced in *House of Small Shadows*, filling the corridors outside Catherine's room and also, most overtly – and to the greatest narrative effect – in *No One Gets Out Alive*, where the spirits of the departed speak to Steph, communicating with her directly about the dangers of 82 Edgehill Rd.

Indeed, the voices are there right from the beginning and even appear in the opening chapter. The same chapter also introduces another sound which will take on huge significance as the novel progresses. When Steph hears the sound of polythene rustling, she attributes it to mice chewing on the material. The actual explanation for the source of the noise turns out to be far more disturbing than that.

The recording of strange sounds also features in Adam's novels, the playback of the recordings adding an extra frisson of horror to them, infiltrating the "safe" environment in which they are being replayed. There's

---

[28] Another impressive filmic use of dogs barking off screen is in Ari Aster's Hereditary following the séance in the Grahams' house. The sound occurs at the end of the scene then carries over into the next.

something about hearing unexpected sounds or noises that strikes right into the fear response, an out of place sob, growl or voice will immediately have the goosebumps breaking out, initiating that delightful trickle of ice water down the spine.

At one point in *Last Days*, Kyle Freeman recalls some accidental sound effects he's picked up on previous documentary filming projects, the "ocean" sound of the huge forest featured in *Blood Frenzy* and strange, subterranean noises whilst filming in Scotland for *Coven*. The films are of course self-referential, *Blood Frenzy* tells the story of *The Ritual* whilst *Coven* is based on the events of *Banquet For The Damned*, the latter of which features its own sound recordings in which Beth channels the voice of the ancient witch who has possessed her[29].

Possibly the most significant recordings to be found in all of the novels are those of Lincoln, the brother of Helene in *The Reddening*. Recorded in the area around the lair of Old Creel, it is these recordings which are the impetus for Helene to travel to the south coast as she investigates what happened to her brother before his suicide.

It's another stand-out sequence of the novels in which the contents of the recordings are described: Thunder, air whistling through a pipe, voices, thumps, infants crying, barks and bestial shrieks, hisses and growls and, to finish things off, a high-pitched laugh[30].

---

[29] *Last Days* also features a scene in which Kyle reviews a recording of one of the interviews he has just completed. The camera had been left running whilst he and his partner Dan fled the building and it's what he sees on the "found footage" on the reclaimed camera that produces a scene which I regard as one of the best ever written in the horror genre.

[30] Not recorded, but present in the actual caverns themselves, is the sound of trickling water – another Nevill favourite which also appears in *Under A Watchful Eye* and *Cunning Folk*.

Sound is not the only way in which Adam Nevill assaults the readers' senses. As well as stimulating the auditory pathways he takes aim at the olfactory nerves too.

Smell has been shown to be one of the most potent stimuli for releasing memories and eliciting emotional responses. This phenomenon is called the Proust Effect, courtesy of Marcel Proust and his seven volume novel *À la Recherche du Temps Perdu*, in particular what has become known as the "episode of the madeleine" in which the unnamed narrator partakes of the eponymous cake and at once experiences an involuntary memory of eating the same snack as a child.

Science provides the rationale for this; the olfactory centres of the brain are closely associated with the limbic system which is responsible for generating emotion and memory, a physical connection which creates the sudden flashbacks we have all experienced when we smell a specific odour[31].

Given art is all about creating emotional responses it would seem reasonable to attempt to somehow use smells and aromas to do so. Cinema has tried in the past with Smell-O-Vision, Smell-O-Rama, AromaRama and Odorama[32] all bursting onto the scene only to wither and die almost immediately.

A variety of odours appear in Adam's books and, like his use of sound, succeed admirably in adding atmospheric flourishes to the narratives. In some instances it's simply enough to mention a well-known aroma to stimulate readers' own experiences of it and thus create an

---

[31] Those connections may be even closer than first realised. Recent research on mice has shown that their olfactory tubercles also respond to sounds. This has created the concept of "smound", a perception generated by a combination of sound and smell.

[32] The last by John Waters no less, in 1982 for his film *Polyester*. The system used scratch and sniff cards to produce the smells.

ambience but the books also contain some marvellously creative descriptions of smells.

Examples of the former are to be found in *House of Small Shadows*, where the aromas of "stale tobacco, brittle paper and polished wood" combine to create a sense of age and antiquity as befits the gothic nature of the Red House. So too the smell of mothballs and camphor which linger around Edith (and in particular her wig) whilst the pungent smells of the chemicals used by M H Mason lend an authentic air to his workshop.

These old and musty aromas are cleverly counterpointed later in the novel when Catherine finally manages to break free from the confines of the Red House[33]. Passing through the grounds, and beyond, she smells the aroma of flowers and freshly-baked bread; pleasant smells much in contrast to the fustiness of the house itself, suggestive of a fresh beginning, a break from the horrors that have gone before.

The use of smell to create atmosphere is also a feature of the opening chapters of *Cunning Folk*. When Tom and his family first enter their new home they're met with a variety of odours from within:

And immediately, deep from the throat, the mouth of the old house breathes on them, gusting a miasma from its mouldering innards.

Among those smells are the acidic stench of animal urine and the gassy whiff of sewage. It's a perfect encapsulation of the smell of an old, empty house, the language and descriptions offering up an intense feeling of foreboding. The paragraph ending with the sublime:

---

[33] Or does she…?

Cold, compressed, autumnal odours; the last spirits to
slope from buildings that have lain empty.

This use of smells to suggest a dark history and/or the presence of something supernatural is also employed in *Apartment 16*. As well as the strange sounds protagonist Seth hears emerging from the rooms in question, he also detects the smell of sulphur and burning. Brimstone and fire is a biblical expression for the wrath of God, (brimstone being an archaic name for sulphur), but the connotations these combined smells imply belong more in the realm of the underworld and the fires of Hades. Indeed, what lies beyond the door of apartment 16 is certainly a lot closer to hell than to heaven.

Bad smells indicate bad places, a notable example being the cottage in *Banquet For The Damned* which is filled with aroma of putrefaction and decay. This is in part due to the evil which has been perpetrated within its walls but also more directly to the paintings found inside, created not with paint but from an assortment of bodily fluids and tissues.

The rank smell of decomposition is the signature fragrance of the Blood Friends in *Last Days* too. It's first experienced by film-makers Kyle and Dan when they return to the London apartment they had fled earlier in order to pick up their equipment. Whilst they might not meet the terrifying creatures at that point, the retrieved camera later reveals exactly what had been in the building with them on their earlier visit.

Just as bad smells are associated with the monsters[34] which lurk within the novels, and their residues, so too is

---

[34] Old Creel's malignant odour precedes him as he approaches along his underground tunnel. An early appearance of the Brown Man in *Banquet For The Damned* is accompanied by the "*stench of a slit whale belly*".

it a shared feature of the bad men who populate their pages. The most extreme example of this is to be found in Ewan, the flatmate from hell who sets into motion the disintegration of protagonist Seb's life in *Under A Watchful Eye*. The premise of a force of entropy called Ewan encroaching upon the ordered existence of a former friend first appeared in Adam's short story *Yellow Teeth*. Whilst the characters in both stories are different people[35], they do share a name, motivation and, above all, a passing acquaintance only with the principles of personal hygiene.

Ewan stinks.

His body odour is industrial strength and is described vividly with phrases bordering on the poetic. He smells like:

Cattle and ethanol with a hint of shellfish left in the sun...
a male groin left too long unwashed...

Whilst Ewan may be regarded as one of the villains of the piece, there's an argument to be made that he is simply misguided, and so obsessed with his grand theories that he is oblivious to the harm his presence is having on Seb's life. In other of Adam's novels however, the link between bad smells and bad character is more definite.

No One Gets Out Alive features two of the most evil men to populate Adam's books: cousins Knacker and Fergal. Both are repugnant human beings and there is little to separate them in terms of how awful they are. Fergal appears the more threatening, towering over everyone and with the threat of violence constantly lurking beneath the surface. It is he who displays the

---

[35] Or are they? *Under A Watchful Eye* is so metafictional that it's not beyond the realms of possibility that they are the same person.

Nevillesque characteristic of smelling bad[36], his odour at one point being described as "sebaceous".

It's a fine word to use. A career in hospital pathology labs exposed me to just about every smell a human body can produce and I can confidently say that the one which emanates from a sebaceous cyst is amongst the worst of them[37].

It's an evocative word for sure, and one which Adam also applies to the smell of the dingy flat belonging to Bowles, one of the paedophiles the Father "interviews" during the search for his daughter in *Lost Girl* and again to describe one of the odours present in the farmhouse that Steve is searching prior to his capture and sacrifice in *The Reddening*.

Animal Magic

The use of animals as characters in literature is well established. Whilst some novels go the full anthropomorphic route and employ the animals as protagonists – Richard Adams' rabbits of *Watership Down* and his eponymous *Plague Dogs* or the moles of William Horwood's *Duncton Wood* series – others present them realistically and naturally, such as in the novels of Gavin Maxwell and Jack London. And then there are those who employ creatures in supporting, albeit important, roles, often using the same animals in different novels. After *Setting Free the Bears* in his debut novel, John Irving managed to shoehorn his ursine characters into a number of his subsequent books, irrespective of the

---

[36] A trait he shares with former owner/landlord Bennet, his distinctive aroma an indication of the presence of his ghost in the corridor outside Steph's room.

[37] Imagine vinegar combined with shit and you won't be far off.

41

locations in which they were set. Similarly, it seemed for a time that Dean Koontz must have somehow been contractually obliged to feature a Golden Retriever in his novels, usually ones with some kind of psychic ability.

Whilst animals do make an appearance in Adam's books, it's most frequently as monstrous versions of themselves, either directly as flesh and blood, red-in-tooth-and-claw adversaries, or as simulacra or points of reference; imagery displayed in paintings, sculptures and masks. In doing so, he's carrying on a long tradition of using our bestial companions in a horror setting.

Canines have a well-established association with horror[38]. Among many, many examples are *The Hound of the Baskervilles*[39], Dracula's "children of the night" making their sweet music and, of course, Stephen King's *Cujo*. In film too our doggy companions have made a number of notable appearances including the rottweilers of *The Omen* that carry out the cemetery attack (and also provide the hellhound companion for Damien) and Jed, the husky whose escape from the Norwegian camp brings untold horrors to Antarctic Research Station Outpost #31.

Edith Mason, the resident of the Red House in *House of Small Shadows* has a pet dog, a Red Setter, which makes a brief appearance but a more disturbing canine is to be found in one of the taxidermy tableaux created by her uncle. When Catherine is shown the "nursery" exhibit, one of the beds occupied by a variety of stuffed animals has a dog's muzzle protruding from beneath the covers, the preserved head topped by a sun bonnet from which chestnut curls tumble. Later on in the book, when Catherine is made to watch the grainy film of the cruelty

---

[38] You might say they have a long pedigree.

[39] Which absolutely is a gothic horror story, and evidence that the crossover between crime and horror fiction is not a recent development.

play, a recreation of the martyrdom of Henry Strader using puppets and marionettes, the "Master of Revels" who introduces proceedings has the hind legs of a dog.

The dogs of *Last Days* have already been mentioned, the sound of their barking a backdrop to events on the Arizona ranch. The animals themselves have a key role in proceedings during the Ascent, providing homes for the translocated souls of (some of) the participants but the novel which features dogs most prominently is *The Reddening*.

As previously stated, Old Creel – the ancient creature worshipped by the Red People – is of canine descent, so too its white pups, the offspring which dwell alongside it in their underground lair, terrifying creatures as big as bears and which walk upon their hind legs.

There's a scene early in the book in which Helene, retracing the steps of her missing brother, stumbles onto some private land and is attacked by dogs – big, sinewy beasts that are most likely Dobermans – that nicely foreshadows the supernatural horrors to come and which fits perfectly into the canine motif of the novel.

1973 saw the release of one of the greatest horror films of all time[40], *The Exorcist*. In what was obviously a standout year for horror cinema, *Pigs* was also released, a movie which failed to reach the dizzy heights of William Friedkin's masterpiece in terms of popularity or critical acclaim [41]– something which no doubt prompted the film's producer to shoot extra scenes involving possession and exorcism (despite them having nothing to do with the plot) and re-releasing the film under a new title. It's a

---

[40] If not one of the greatest films of all time.

[41] This despite free bacon being handed out to the audience attending the premiere.

ploy that made no difference whatsoever, although their determination to make the film a success has so far resulted in it being re-edited and renamed a further twelve times.

All of which useless trivia serves to introduce the second animal to make regular appearances in Adam's novels: the pig. Pigs in literature tend to be of the benign persuasion but Napoleon and his cohorts are definitely the villains of the piece in Orwell's *Animal Farm* (or at the very least proof that power corrupts). *The Lord of the Flies* in William Golding's novel is a pig's head of course[42] and as far as horror is concerned, some prime examples are the swine creature from William Hope Hodgson's *The House on the Borderland* and Jodie, the terrifying red-eyed pig who appears outside the windows of the house in *The Amityville Horror*.

Ignoring *Pigs* for now[43], porcine horrors in film have been relatively limited. Jodie does make an appearance in the movie version of *The Amityville Horror* (but is as much of a let-down as the film as a whole is) and a mutant pig wreaks havoc in the Korean film *Chaw* – a similar scenario to that of the Australian film *Razorback*.

The antipodean location of the latter is shared by the story in which an early incarnation of Nevillesque porcine horrors appear: the New Zealand-set *Pig Thing*. In it, young siblings are terrorised by the titular beast, an ancient creature closely associated with the landscape in which it lives and who is undoubtedly a precursor of both Moder and Old Creel.

The latter's canine provenance has already been established but one of the men who kidnap and then

---

[42] And the character Piggy comes to a pretty horrific end.

[43] Something cinema-goers have been doing for the best part of fifty years.

attempt to drown Helene in *The Reddening* is described as pig-like in appearance, an allusion to the less desirable characteristics of the species and certainly not their huge intelligence.[44]

Among the many animal masks donned by various characters in a number of Adam's novels is the pig-mask worn by Medea Moot when she participates in the bizarre forest glade rituals with her brother Magi. That mask is of course a representation of the god they both worship and hold captive: the Sow Beneath the Earth. Like Moder then, this is a female deity but, unlike the Scandinavian monster, is not free to roam the landscape and wreak havoc, is kept in check by the activities of the Moots; something which adds an ironic twist to the culmination of events in the novel, the realisation that trying to do good often makes things worse. The horror of the Sow lies in her potential for the death and destruction as so vividly described in both *The Ritual* and *The Reddening*.

My personal favourite of the Nevill pigs – by which I mean the one I find most unsettling and scary - doesn't actually appear in person at all and is found within the pages of *Last Days*. When protagonist Kyle Freeman takes a trip to Antwerp, he is shown a triptych of paintings by Niclaes Verhulst called *The Saints of Filth*. The painting is kept under lock and key, hidden away from the public as a precautionary measure – some who have viewed it have been driven mad by the experience.

The triptych depicts events from the sixteenth century in which Konrad Lorche and his devoted followers (an earlier incarnation of Sister Katherine and the Temple of the Last Days) are persecuted and martyred, finally escaping the mortal world in the ritual of the Ascent.

---

[44] Similarly, in *No One Gets Out Alive*, upon hearing the sounds of sex from the room above, Steph imagines the man as pig-like, with a red face and black-haired flanks.

The scene in which the triptych is described is hugely powerful, dripping in atmosphere and evoking images of the paintings of Heironymous Bosch and some of the more fantastic works of Breugel the Elder. Kyle's viewing of the paintings brings about feelings of light-headedness and discomfiture and because the writing is so good those emotions are shared by the reader. Most striking of all the images is that of the wonderfully named Unholy Swine – Lorche's bishop, a pig pictured sitting upon a throne, ascending to a raging maelstrom in the sky, a copy of Lorche's manifesto clutched in one trotter. He is joined in his ascent by a pack of dogs, raised upon their hind legs (just like Old Creel's pups) who frolic among the Blood Friends in the troubled skies above the city.

Despite only occupying a few lines in the novel, the Unholy Swine still manages to make a huge impact, the unease and discomfort such anthropomorphic creations elicit adding to the power of what is already a truly striking image.

If a dog and a pig occupy the first two panels of the Nevill menagerie triptych, then the third belongs to the hare. Whilst the 1972 epic *Night of the Lepus* proved that members of the eponymous genus are not, in themselves, particularly scary[45], hares have a long association with folkloric traditions.

As well as being a favourite animal into which to transform by witches, they are closely linked to the Sidh, or fairies, of Irish folklore and are regarded as tricksters in African cultures. Their exuberant displays during the breeding season has given rise to the phrase "mad as a march hare", the dancing/boxing they perform a

---

[45] Although the Killer Rabbit of Caerbannog would probably disagree with this statement.

manifestation of their high libidos, a characteristic that once made them the perfect gift from a suitor[46].

The symbolic image of the three hares is an ancient one, depicting three of the animals chasing each other in a circle, their ears touching in the centre and has been appropriated by the Christian church to represent the Holy Trinity – a far cry from its original association with fertility rites – and in Britain, the legend of the White Hare describes the reincarnation of a vengeful female spirit in the body of the eponymous beast in order to hunt down the man who betrayed her[47].

Hares have featured less frequently than their rabbit cousins in fiction, (although Br'er rabbit is based on the trickster hare of African folklore, the original stories making their way to America's deep south by way of the slave trade). The aforementioned Mad March Hare makes a significant appearance in *Alice's Adventures in Wonderland* alongside his friend the Hatter and the daemon chosen by Lee Scoresby in Phillip Pulman's *His Dark Materials* is Hester, an Arctic Hare.

With regards visual media, perhaps the most significant appearance of a hare in horror films is the carcass found in the grave where missing girl [48]Rowan is supposed to buried in *The Wicker Man* whilst the TV series *Inside No. 9* features a hare – usually a figurine, but not always – in every episode[49].

Truly the most disturbing hare in television history is, however, Hartley Hare – a puppet character in the

---

[46] Alive, not in a pie.

[47] And provides the title and subject matter of a haunting song by Seth Lakeman. Just listening to it will transport you to the wilds of Dartmoor.

[48] Or "Lost Girl" to stay on brand.

[49] There's fun to be had trying to spot the hare but it's usually a case of "oh, I forgot to look" come the end of each episode.

children's show *Pipkins* which aired between 1973[50] and 1981. Countless childhoods must have been scarred by exposure to this bizarre creature, further traumatising psyches already damaged by the terrifying doll Hamble[51] who haunted the studios of *Play School*. It's a theory of mine that both these monsters affected Adam at an impressionable age and that his novel *House of Small Shadows* – in which both puppets and dolls feature heavily - is his way of exorcising those particular demons.

That novel does feature a hare among the menagerie of taxidermy on display inside the Red House. In the same nursery tableau in which the dog mentioned earlier appears, a resident of one of the other tiny beds is indeed a hare. Later in the book, the grainy film of the cruelty play that Catherine is forced to watch includes a sequence in which the instigator of the trial which will lead to the conviction and martyrdom of Henry Stader is played by the marionette of a hare. This bears a striking similarity to J.T. Holden's 2010 reimagining of Alice's *Adventures in Wonderland*, his extended poem *Alice in Verse: The Lost Rhymes of Wonderland*. As with the original, the Mad March Hare appears although whereas the animal was little more than a witness for the prosecution in Caroll's book, he is here the chief prosecutor.

There's another, indirect reference to hares within *House of Small Shadows* when Catherine first encounters the nursery tableau and has a memory of a marionette with thin, furred legs and long ears on a children's TV

---

[50] Which, as already ascertained, was a fine year for horror being that in which *Pigs* was released. And *The Exorcist*.

[51] Legend has it, that one of the presenters rammed a knitting needle through Hamble's body. The reason given was that it would provide support as the doll was unable to sit up on her own and *not* an attempt to kill what was, essentially, evil incarnate.

programme which struck her as sinister, that feeling persisting to the present day.

In *Cunning Folk*, Magi Moot dons a hare mask when participating in the bizarre rituals he joins his sister Medea in and it's into that animal he transforms as the magic they conjure between them takes over.

The same kind of mask is worn in *The Ritual* by Surtr, the female member of Blood Frenzy. The mask itself is a horrifying creation:

...tatty brownish fur sprung in clumps from a long face... two long pillars of discoloured bone dripped from its dirty black mouth...

It's an interesting choice of animal for a mask. Fenris and Loki, the other members of Blood Frenzy wear representations of a goat and a lamb, both caprines in keeping with the provenance of Moder herself. That a hare should be included only serves to reinforce how closely connected they are to folk mythology traditions.

As with *Inside No. 9*, the hares in Adam's novels are often hard to spot. In *The Reddening*, they are relegated to the skeletal remains of its Arctic species which are reported as having been found during excavations of the prehistoric site at the beginning of the novel but the most subtle of them all has to be in *No One Gets Out Alive* in which protagonist Steph, upon escaping from 82 Edgehill Road, carves out a new life and existence with a new name: Amber Hare[52].

---

[52] A transformation into a hare that doesn't involve witchcraft.

Nightmares and Dreamscapes

Dreams are a commonly used literary device and can be employed in a variety of ways. Given that they are an accumulation of memories, the outcome of the brain's attempt to process and record them, pages of clunky exposition or the sudden appearance of a flashback can be avoided simply by having a character dream of past events. As well as the past, they can also evoke the present emotional state of a character and, moving to the other end of the time spectrum, can also serve as premonitions, foreshadowing events still to come.

The trope of "It was all a dream" as a dénouement is rightly frowned upon nowadays, relegated to the ranks of Bad Cliches That Must Never Be Used, and regarded as little more than a cop-out. Its usage within the body of the text however is less problematical, indeed can serve to enhance atmosphere and wrong-foot the reader, making them question what is real and what isn't, and as such is often deployed in horror fiction whose aim, after all, is to unsettle.

The ancient belief that dreams were actually the result of the soul leaving the body is another facet of them which is used to good effect within horror - a genre better placed than mainstream fiction to exploit the slightly outré nature of the concept. This allows characters to discover information relevant to the plot that would otherwise not be available to them.

Dreams feature in all of Adam's novels, used in a variety of ways and, indeed, are a key component to the plot of his debut *Banquet For The Damned*. Hart Miller, an American Visiting Doctor of Anthropology, is researching the nightmares that are plaguing the student body at St Andrews.

These night terrors are more than just dreams of course, are actual visitations by the entity known as the Brown Man, a familiar summoned by the reawakened coven practicing in the town[53]. During one of his interviews with one of the unfortunate students, (although fortunate enough to escape the clutches of the Brown Man), Miller has this to say about night terrors:

"Well, when a locale has a long tradition of superstition, and if the roots of that history are deeply entrenched in the occult, sleepers often suffer the same nightmares for generations."

This concept of locations influencing the dreams of characters is employed in a number of the novels. When Luke and his companions first become lost in the Scandinavian forest in *The Ritual*, the relief they feel at discovering a cabin in which to spend the night is immediately replaced by apprehension once they find what lurks within and ultimately by fear and panic the next morning after they all experience terrifying nightmares[54].

Only Luke's nightmare is described as it happens, (Hutch's pops up a little later on in the narrative), but provides plenty of foreshadowing; he finds himself stumbling through the dark woods – recollections of actual events – before being confronted by the image of a horned beast which proceeds to attack him. Up to this point, Moder has not been seen, only her aftermath, the

---

[53] Which does bear some resemblance to the *modus operandum* of Freddy Krueger. Interestingly, there is an Elm Street in St Andrews. Unfortunately, it's St Andrews, Manitoba not St Andrews, Fife.

[54] In a nice touch, the last line of the chapter preceding Luke's nightmare is a line of dialogue, "Sure. Sweet dreams"

implication being that the visions Luke sees in his nightmare are being provided by the location in which he sleeps, past events which have occurred there still resonating, strongly enough to penetrate the subconscious mind of anyone who finds themselves present there. As Dante, protagonist of *Banquet For The Damned*, remarks at one point,

"The dreams are like a prelude, an introduction to something."

It's the Stone Tape theory in action, and reiterates the theory postulated by Hart Miller in the quote above. It's a manifestation too of the gothic trope of the past impacting on the present. A similar scenario is seen in the opening chapters of *Cunning Folk* in which the whole family suffer bad dreams on their first night in the new house – its cursed nature overcoming any feelings of excitement and joy at moving in. Or perhaps it's the entire village of Eadric which exerts this malign influence over its residents. Whilst *Cunning Folk* was set nearby, Nerthus House, the prime location in *The Vessel* is situated directly in its centre and yes, protagonist Jess is plagued by bad dreams on the nights she spends there[55], fusions of current concerns mixed in with echoes of horrific past events at the vicarage.

Katrine's interview with paraglider Matt in *The Reddening* uncovers the fact that he is suffering from nightmares too – the reason for which he places fairly and squarely on the caves beneath the ground that are the lair of Old Creel. There's evidence too that he is not the only one to suffer, that anyone in proximity to the locale is

---

[55] Including a fine example of a dream within a dream a la *American Werewolf in London*. (But very different to Edgar Allan Poe's).

susceptible; two of the archaeologists working on the dig killed themselves, as did Katrine's brother whose sound recordings in the caves brought her to the region in the first place.

Having those malevolent echoes of past events concentrated within the confines of a single building provides nightmare fuel for joint protagonists Apryl and Seth in *Apartment 16*. Of the two, it's Seth who is most affected, his early dreams of being held in an isolated prison (the "chamber") transforming into far worse visions, glimpses inside the titular apartment alongside a ghostly, hooded companion, there to witness the horrors and grotesqueries within. As his exposure to it increases, so the building's influence on him extends beyond its confines, at one point creating a vision of hell in a branch of Sainsbury's. Most disturbingly of all, the visions are no longer confined to his sleep but have begun to infiltrate his waking hours as well.

Steph, trapped within 82 Edgehill Rd, also suffers from disturbed sleep, visited as she is by the ghosts of previous tenants in *No One Gets Out Alive*. Although presented as dreams, these encounters are actually happening – the ghosts are real – but it's clever writing to sow the seeds of doubt in readers' minds, deftly employing the "is it real?" technique.

This blurring of the lines between dreamscapes and reality is also employed in *House of Small Shadows*. During the early stages of her confinement in the Red House, Catherine's dreams are of the regular variety, recollections of past events which nicely serve to create backstory but as the weirdness she is exposed to grows ever stronger she descends into a kind of limbo where time becomes fluid and no one, Catherine or the reader, is entirely sure of what is real and what isn't.

In *Under A Watchful Eye*, one of the first appearances of Thin Len, the malevolent spirit unleashed as a result of M L Hazzard's "research" is presented as a dream – one shared by protagonist Seb and his girlfriend Vicky. The fact that they both dream about the same thing of course suggests that the events did actually happen; that Seb is now haunted. This is a different kind of haunting to those in the other novels however. Whereas it was the locations the protagonists found themselves in that contained the restless spirits, this haunting occurs long before Seb goes anywhere near Hunter's Tor. The reason Thin Len is sniffing around is Ewan, Seb's housemate from hell; his re-entry into Seb's life has brought Len too, following him around like a shadow.

Indeed, it's not long after Ewan arrives that Seb's bad dreams begin, including one which may well be a veiled reference to *Banquet For The Dead*, featuring as it does a skeletal figure scuttling across a golf course. Descriptions of subsequent dreams reveal that they are actually premonitions, the malign influence that Ewan has brought with him allowing Seb glimpses of the horrors that lie in wait for him.

It's perhaps because the remaining two novels feature protagonists who are following their own prescribed courses of action, rather than being unwittingly placed in horrifying environments[56], that dreams feature less prominently in the narratives.

In *Lost Girl*, it's not even the Father but Oleg, the shaman and member of the Kings gang who has a dream worthy of note. It's a hugely significant one though, in which he foresees the coming of the Father, thereby lending the protagonist an air of heroic mystique, a

---

[56] Something explored in more detail in Chapter Three.

suggestion that some kind of supernatural force – or maybe fate or destiny - is guiding his actions.

Given the sights he witnesses, it's unsurprising that Kyle Freeman finds himself suffering nightmares as he hunts down the legacy of Sister Katherine and her cult in *Last Days*. His dreams contain a strange amalgam of images but are suggestive of an overstimulated imagination responding to information he has already discovered rather than any supernatural or precognitive abilities on Kyle's part.

A recurring image is of burnt remains and sooty faces – no doubt a reference to the fire that destroys the Arizona home of the cult, and one of barking children has a direct correlation to the events which unfolded on its last night. Others are harder to tie in though, but perhaps

Swine bellows and guttural bleats… from shaky jowls and a large mouth. A black tongue and yellow teeth. Wet, close…

could refer to Moder from *The Ritual*. Prior to his investigation of the Temple of the Last Days, Kyle had made a film, *Blood Frenzy*, about the disappearance of a group of hikers in the forests of Northern Scandinavia.
Even more intriguingly, the description of figures who are

Stripped, lean and smeared ruddy…

could be a reference to the cult of Old Creel as featured in *The Reddening* – a novel written some seven years after *Last Days*. Evidence, perhaps, of a premonition for the author himself...

Dark Morbidities

Behavioural evolution has resulted in humans being hardwired to regard creatures with angular morphologies as a threat, something to be feared whilst those with rounded features are seen as attractive and friendly. As a rule of thumb it's a pretty good one; to be an effective predator requires long limbs for locomotion and sharp, pointy bits to inflict damage and, conversely, the exaggeratedly large round eyes of young animals have evolved specifically to generate feelings of empathy in order that they will be fed and nurtured rather than attacked.

These basic instincts are coloured by cultural factors when the creatures being assessed are other human beings. Whilst the tall, thin ectomorphic body is perfectly natural, when taken to extremes it can conjure up thoughts and fears of illness and the wasting away of tissue presaging death, for many the greatest fear of all. Such emaciated individuals can be described as cadaverous, a direct comparison to dead bodies.

It's little surprise then that the wasted form provides the template for so many creatures – supernatural and otherwise – found in the realms of horror fiction.

Skeletons, of course, are traditional fare for horror stories – the personification of death is itself a robed skeleton – but are so well established as to have now become a cliché[57]. A thin covering of skin somehow makes them a whole lot scarier, and it's a look that has been employed to great effect when imagining both living

---

[57] The last time I was impressed by skeletons in a film was in 1982's *Poltergeist* when they emerged from the swimming pool and looked genuinely terrifying. They were actually real skeletons, not dummy props, and this "misuse" of human remains is regarded by some as the reason behind the supposed "curse" of the film.

and undead monsters, F W Murnau's *Nosferatu* is undeniably far more terrifying to regard than the devilishly handsome Count Dracula.

The emaciated and cadaverous are a recurring motif in Adam's novels, and indeed appear in his debut novel *Banquet For The Damned*. The Brown Man, the demon familiar of the coven in St Andrews is a huge – taller than two men – figure dressed in ragged robes, his true morphology never fully seen but with long limbs and fingers, his every movement generating the sound of cracks and rustles, the clacking of bones.

When Felix Hessen finally makes an appearance at the end of *Apartment 16*, he's described as having arms

...so long and thin they must have been bone.

It's a description that also fits King Death, the deity worshipped by the Kings in *Lost Girl*. Whilst never appearing "in person" in the novel, he still manages to haunt proceedings with his image painted graffiti-like on buildings and walls[58].

When Luke is taken up to the loft of the house in which he is being held captive in *The Ritual*, what he finds there provides another marvellously unsettling set piece which drips with atmosphere. Here are kept the mummified remains of the "ancient ones", centuries-old worshippers of Moder, collected together in an unholy shrine. Dressed in dark raiment, tattered cloth similar to that of the Brown Man, they have

Hairless heads… parchment faces… lipless grimaces…
papery eyes

---

[58] Imagery which put me in mind of the blast shadows created by the atomic bomb detonation in Hiroshima.

some propped up against the walls, others piled into caskets; two of them sitting on small chairs in a place of prominence.

It's a hugely effective scene that bores directly into all those fears of death and decay[59] that reside in our reptile brains. A disturbing scenario that then becomes even more so when the whispering starts and the bodies begin to move…

Given how metafictional it is, I wouldn't be surprised if the train journey sequence in *Under A Watchful Eye* is a homage to the loft scene, featuring as it does an entity with a

> *pallid scalp stained by large, black moles from which sketchy fronds of dead hair protrude*

which, despite the impression of being dead and decayed is very much alive, and of course there's Thin Len himself, whose very name indicates his most striking physical characteristic.

The most terrifying of all Adam's monsters – in my opinion – are the *Blood Friends* of Last Days. Acolytes of the Unholy Swine, they are a constant threat to Kyle Freeman as he attempts to make his film about the Temple of the Last Days. Similar to Tolkien's Nazgûl, they hunt down the last remaining members of the cult and Kyle's involvement in their story brings him into much closer contact with them than he would like.

Their terrifying appearance is revealed in a brilliantly written scene in which Kyle reviews footage recorded by the camera he abandoned whilst fleeing from an interview and later retrieved. The "found footage" he watches

---

[59] Thanatophobia and seplophobia respectively.

shows exactly what it was that was sharing space with him whilst he was in the building. The writing here is top notch, with the reader feeling the same sense of shock and horror Kyle does as the evidence unfolds before him. It's horror by remove, and hugely effective with the descriptions of the Blood Friend that wanders in front of the lens pitch-perfect.

A pair of haggard legs beneath a shrivelled groin. And the insinuation… of wasted buttocks. Flesh bleached like a whale's belly. The knee bones were pinched, the calves stringy, the ankle and heels more bone than tissue… the foot was long and pointed… fleshless.

It's not only the supernatural creatures which lurk within the pages of these novels who inhabit these emaciated frames, some of the human characters share similar morphologies. Magi Moot, warlock-in-residence in *Cunning Folk* certainly fits into this category as does the wheelchair-bound witch-mother in *The Reddening*.

Whereas for both of these, their skeletal forms are their natural ones – with age a contributing factor – there are others for whom the degeneration of their bodies has been brought about by exposure to malign forces, both human and supernatural.

When Steph begins her ordeal in the basement flat of 82 Edgehill Rd in *No One Gets Out Alive*, among the parade of ghastly images she encounters there is the body of Bennet, the previous owner of the house. Long dead, the process of decomposition has not progressed far enough that he is unrecognisable with his eyes

…magnified through the lenses of his glasses… collapse(d) into the sockets to resemble the dried-out bodies of dead snails

and his body shrunk to be "unappealingly thin" within the dark suit he wears.

In Bennet's case, the wasting of his body is of course post mortem but in *Banquet For The Damned* academic Eliot Coldwell is reduced to skeletal proportions while he is still alive. When Dante is searching for his friend Tom, he enters the cottage belonging to Coldwell, and finds the tenant cowering in an upstairs room.

> *A bundle of pink sticks, gnarled and grey-headed,*
> *shrunken on the bare boards, unclean...*

Coldwell has been held captive by Beth but the implication is that his degeneration is not simply due to lack of food but also to torture and through being exposed to the evil which now fills the house as a result of the activities performed within it. Indeed, after his first encounter with Beth, Dante himself immediately falls ill, so powerful is the malign atmosphere that surrounds her.

A similar deterioration is seen in Matt, the paraglider who accidentally falls under the eye of the red people in *The Reddening*. Paranoia and nightmares along with actual threats from the cult have reduced the previously outgoing, fit man to a shadow of his former self.

> *Redrawn as worn and sticklike... the sleeves of his shirt*
> *now sagged from a pair of wasted arms.*

Dreams in which they appear as emaciated and skeletal versions of themselves are shared by Kyle in *Last Days* and Seb in *Under A Watchful Eye*. The latter of course has the human manifestation of waste and decay thrust upon him in the form of Ewan.

As mentioned previously, the character of Ewan, and the premise of the housemate from hell, originated in Adam's short story *Yellow Teeth*[60] (which also provides the title of Part One of the novel). It's a descriptor applied to Ewan himself as Seb recollects his university days and his first encounter with his tormentor but is to be found in a number of Adam's other books too.

Moder in *The Ritual* has them, as does Fergal, Knacker's cousin and co-nemesis of Steph in *No One Gets Out Alive*. Luteal dentition is also to be found in the Brown Man of *Banquet For The Damned* and the dog mask worn by the witch-mother in *The Reddening*[61]. They also make fleeting appearances in the visions of the Vortex in *Apartment 16* as well as Seth's recollections of a baboon which sported them.

The most recent Nevill creation to sport yellow teeth is Flo Gardner, resident of Nerthus House in *The Vessel*. Flo, of course, is very old and this is the reason for the bad teeth and wizened appearance which place her firmly in this section. Gerontophobia can be fancily described as the fear of age-related self-degeneration or more bluntly as a fear of old people. It stems from the fear of death – old people are closer to that milestone than the rest of us, and the physical changes wrought in them by the ageing process are a reminder of the fate that awaits us all.

Scary old people are a fixture of the horror genre and Flo is a fine addition to their ranks. The horror in *The Vessel* comes not so much from her physical appearance however, rather her unsettling – to say the least – behaviour, capable as she is of shockingly sudden

---

[60] And which undoubtedly also provided the inspiration for the character of Rick, the slovenly housemate of Jason, who comes to a very sticky end in *Banquet For The Damned*.

[61] As well as in the neanderthal skulls unearthed from the caves in the same book.

outbursts, psychological manipulation and paranormal acts of physical prowess.

Edith Mason, in *House of Small Shadows* is another scary old person gracing the pages of Adam's books. Her powdered wigs might hide the thinning hair on her head but not the malign intent beneath her outwardly benign nature.

The most disturbing Nevill elders however, are undoubtedly the Shafers in *Apartment 16*. In reality, all of the elderly residents in Barrington House are a bit weird but these two claim the title of creepiest by virtue of a terrific sequence early in the book in which they feature in a waking dream/nightmare of nightwatchman Seth.

They appear as grotesque versions of themselves. Whilst Mrs Shafer tends more towards the glutinous, visceral horrors favoured by Lovecraftian fiction, Mr Shafer embodies all the degenerative qualities of gerontophobic disquiet; all wizened limbs with protruding ribs and hollow pelvis, he is at one point described as

The skeleton of a dead child taking its first unholy steps around a crypt...

Now there's an image to contemplate.

Returning to the thoughts on behavioural evolution that opened this section, whilst some of the fear engendered by creatures such as insects, crustaceans and - in particular - spiders is their angular shape, another part comes from the way they move, often quickly and unexpectedly. Given Adam's propensity for mining the primal fears of readers, it's no surprise that he uses this kinetophobia in a number of his novels.

Moving Experiences

The scuttling, skittering movement like that displayed by spiders and crustaceans is unsettling enough in its own right but when it is exhibited by larger organisms it can be downright terrifying. Whereas such motion is natural and normal for those particular invertebrates, when a person – or person-shaped supernatural entity – does the same the disturbing effect is magnified by the sheer inappropriateness of the movements.

The tall, thin figure which plagues the night terrors of the students in *Banquet For The Damned* sets the precedent for similar creatures which appear in Adam's subsequent novels. Indeed, it's the Brown Man's movement which catches the eye of the victims, dropping to all fours and "scuttling like a crab". Given the Brown Man is *very* tall, the image this conjures is a truly disturbing one.

Thin Len, of *Under A Watchful Eye*, has a similar physiognomy to the Brown Man and shares many of his locomotory traits. A brilliant set-piece on a train has him pursuing protagonist Seb, the claustrophobia engendered by the cramped carriages magnifying the horror of his relentless approach. Earlier in the book he is heard by both Seb and Becky in their shared "dream", crawling across the outside walls of the house. This only adds to the arachnoid nature of the entity, able to cling onto vertical surfaces and scuttle across them[62].

Whilst Len is heard but not seen in his nocturnal scramblings, readers are treated to a full view of this wall-

---

[62] Among many other examples, reading this scene put me in mind of the old woman crawling along the ceiling of the psychiatric ward in *Exorcist III*.

clinging activity in *The Vessel*. Here, the frightening free-climber is Flo Gardner herself, her paranormally athletic abilities lent even more horrific impact by the fact of her age and that she is normally semi-comatose and confined to a wheelchair.

The transformation of biped to quadruped in order to crawl across vertical surfaces is something employed on the ground too by various Nevillesque entities. The aforementioned Brown Man and Thin Len both exhibit this behaviour in pursuit of their victims and it's also something which Magi and Medea Moot incorporate into their backward dancing routines as part of their ritualistic worship of The Sow Beneath the Earth in *Cunning Folk*. This is a prelude to their actual transformation into animals of course, Magi to a hare and Medea into a boar; bizarre enough but not as much as a similar scenario in *Last Days*. In the course of his investigations, Kyle Freeman uncovers footage of the now grown-up children who escaped the massacre at the Arizona home of the Temple of the Last Days. The film shows them running around on all fours, tongues lolling, surrounded by dog toys, sniffing and barking. It's a truly disturbing image, enhanced by its description of having been taken from a distance; shaky, hand-held footage which has intruded upon a dark secret.

The inverse scenario, quadrupeds walking on their hind legs, is just as disturbing. A huge part of what makes werewolves so terrifying is the way they walk on their hind legs[63] and that imagery also appears within the Nevill novels; the aforementioned triptych in *Last Days* depicts dogs raised onto their hind legs cavorting with the

---

[63] But I still do love *An American Werewolf in London* even though its titular monster remains on all fours.

Blood Friends and in *The Reddening*, Old Creel's white pups are bipedal.

Another abnormal movement to feature in Adam's books is levitation. The ultimate aim of the Temple of the Last Days is the Ascent, the rising up into another plane of existence of Sister Katherine and her followers and once again it's the painting in Antwerp that provides a vivid description of the process, complete with Unholy Swine, barking dogs and Blood Friends.

It's Flo Gardner in *The Vessel* again, who exhibits this paranormal activity to the fullest extent, most dramatically in a scene near the end of the book in which things between Jess and her ex, Tony, come to a head.

In this discussion of the horror inducing effect of "abnormal" movement, it would be remiss not to mention *House of Small Shadows*. The unnerving effect of the anthropomorphic taxidermy tableaux within the Red House has already been mentioned but the book also plays into the primal fears of dolls and puppets, in particular marionettes[64].

This pediophobia is first awakened in an early scene in which protagonist Catherine attends a meeting in a village pub. The room in which the meeting is to take place is full of antique dolls, an already creepy situation made worse by the fact that the man she is supposed to meet there doesn't turn up. Disturbing as they are, the dolls pale in comparison to the marionettes which feature in the film of the cruelty play which Catherine is forced to watch by Edith Mason.

Catherine's dislike of puppets and the way they move has already been mentioned earlier in the novel:

---

[64] The horrors of Hamble have already been discussed but special mention has to be made of the terrifying puppet in Matthew Holness' film *Possum*; a creation that achieves a double whammy by having a terrifying face and arachnoid limbs.

As a child she had always been nervous when a puppet first moved, that lazy uncoordinated wobble when a marionette rose from being seated to standing, or the sway before a puppet leapt about a stage.

The disturbing nature of the film is as much to do with the jerky movements of the marionettes as it does its distressing subject matter. The reactions it brings about in the reader as well as Catherine is a manifestation of automotonophobia, an adjunct to the uncanny valley that simulacra take us into; that pre-existing uneasiness exacerbated by the close-to-but-not-quite authentic movement of the representations themselves[65].

There Will Be Blood

The fear of disease and decay discussed earlier is an example of the disgust component of horror manifesting itself. This emotional response is also tapped into by representations of injury and/or violent death and so it's unsurprising that gore has found a welcoming home in the horror genre.

It seems paradoxical that readers or viewers would willingly subject themselves to scenes of bloody violence but research has shown the physiological response of the body when confronted with gory imagery is the release of endorphins and adrenaline, identical to that which happens when riding a rollercoaster or participating in any activity where there is an element of danger. Added to this is the discovery that disgust has the effect of compelling

---

[65] Readers of a certain age may remember the Judderman adverts for the alcopop Metz featuring both a marionette of the truly scary woodland creature and a 6'5" ballet dancer playing the role chasing a terrified peasant through a snowy forest. I do. In my nightmares.

attention – it's usually the case that when recollecting films the "gory bits" are the ones we remember.

Long before the science was understood, gore has been used as entertainment. The gladiatorial combats in the Coliseum of Ancient Rome and feeding Christians to lions were only part of the show which also included recreations of executions[66] and one of the most famous attractions of fin de siècle Paris was *Le Théâtre du Grand-Guignol* where audiences could watch stage enactments of hammer murders, brain surgery using a chisel and blindings with scissors among other ghoulish acts.

The theatre finally closed its doors in 1962 although business had been tailing off since the end of World War Two. Whilst the Grand Guignol may be gone forever, gore remains a firm fixture in both literary and cinematic horror. Of all the tools available to a horror author, it's perhaps the one that requires the most careful handling. The phrase "less is more" is definitely one to bear in mind when deploying the splatter. Given the body's known responses to such scenes – excitement and innervation – over-usage can lead to the opposite effect to that which may be intended and any horrific impact is lost[67].

Legendary film director Sam Peckinpah made great use of slow motion and exploding blood squibs in his movies, an attempt to depict just how awful it was to be shot but ironically these scenes have a kind of balletic beauty to them, and he ended up creating a cinematic aesthetic that has been widely used (and abused) ever since.

---

[66] Proto-snuff movies.

[67] Which is a criticism levelled at some extreme horror – that it's written and/or filmed to titillate rather than horrify.

Violent, bloody death does feature in Adam's novels and, because the instances in which it occurs don't form a major component of the narratives involved, they retain their ability to shock and horrify.

A technique employed in a few of the novels is to present the aftermath of the violence rather than describing the event itself. This has the joint effect of stimulating readers' imaginations, making them imagine the awful events that have occurred[68] and also giving insight into the perpetrators of the violence – be they human or supernatural – often before they make an appearance themselves; anyone capable of such acts is definitely to be feared.

An early example of this is found in *Banquet For The Damned* in a scene where a severed human arm is found washed up on a beach. Horrific enough for Dante and the others at the scene but even more so for the readers who are privy to the attack of the Brown Man in the opening chapter which has led to the grisly discovery, a scene which ends before the violence begins and are only now given some idea of what actually happened.

A more bloody aftermath is stumbled upon in *Cunning Folk*; the discovery of healer and trainer in magic, A Blackwood PhD, whose dismembered body parts are found strewn around his flat by protagonist Tom:

Every surface is laced red. Blood flecked and streaked as if a leaking body has been spun at speed, in a centrifuge, spilling its liquid and patterning the walls with macabre swirl of graffiti.

---

[68] Something taken to its extreme, and hugely successfully, in the *Wyrd and Other Derelictions* collection.

Any images this chilling scene generates in readers' minds are verified later in the book when Magi Moot meets the same fate as Blackwood, this time the murder is described as it happens in all its gory glory complete with sound effects:

A noisome sound of twisting sinews... a crunch and then a snap... a wet sucking plock...

These events occur late on in the book as the narrative hurtles towards its conclusion but in *The Ritual*, Luke and his companions come across a horrific tableau of violent death in the opening paragraph.

It was the dead thing they found hanging from a tree that changed the trip beyond recognition.

Not just dead, but eviscerated, guts hanging from its opened body. A large animal, torn apart, hanging in a tree – a marvellous introduction to Moder long before she is seen, setting up an impression of size, strength and ferocity as well as intelligence and motivation beyond simply feeding, the body arranged as it is precisely within the branches. The cat and mouse pursuit which makes the first half of the book is given added tension and peril by the knowledge of what the "cat" is capable of, both characters and readers alike aware that as and when the creature strikes there will be no defence against it. This is confirmed in the most gruesome of ways when one of the group is snatched from his tent and then found hanging in a tree with identical injuries to the animal.

It could be argued that Magi's dismemberment in *Cunning Folk* bears resemblance to the ritual killing of Henry Stader as depicted in the cruelty play performed by the marionettes in *House of Small Shadows*. The novel also features a killing reminiscent of the fate of Hutch in *The Ritual* in that disembowelling is involved. As events in the Red House spiral towards their conclusion, Catherine is confronted by the villain of the piece who is naked, masked – and holding a straight razor. This he uses to kill the housekeeper Maude, stabbing the blade into her belly and then tugging

...the razor upwards, like he was trying to free a stuck zipper...

Then, holding her upright with one hand, using the other he

...unspooled the housekeeper into the overgrown grass.

It's a vivid image for sure, conjured up by a wonderful simile and a perfectly innocuous word lent horrific import by the context in which it has been used. Shocking without being gratuitous.

In most of Adam's books, the violence is perpetrated by the "villains" or the supernatural entities which haunt their pages. A notable exception to this is the Father of *Lost Girl* whose systematic despatch of the human monsters involved in the kidnap of his daughter provide milestones on his journey along the path of moral degeneration. He is of course driven by circumstances to commit those acts of violence and the same can be said for Steph in *No One Gets Out Alive*.

The scene in which she kills her captor and tormentor Knacker marks a turning point in the book, a transition from victim to victor. It's a kill or be killed scenario – Knacker is there to make her the latest sacrifice to Black Maggie – and so her retaliation is self-defence but this is also a hugely cathartic moment, a release of the tension

70

and fear that has been her life for the last nine days held captive in 82 Edgehill Rd. She manages to stab Knacker in the throat with a shard of glass and

Only after the glass went in deep, and until her knuckles brushed the stubble on his jawline, did she realise that she was smiling with all of her teeth.

It's fair to say that this feeling of catharsis and elation is shared by readers too. The almost 400 pages which precede this scene have been filled with unrelenting tension. When Steph finally exacts her revenge, and mocks Knacker as he bleeds out on the floor, we're on the sidelines, cheering her on.

The emotions elicited by the violent death of Steve in *The Reddening* are very different however. In all of Adam's books, it's my opinion that this is the most disturbing scene he has written. What makes it so disturbing is not just what happens within it – decapitation, dismemberment and cannibalism – but the matter of fact way in which it is written. Eschewing over the top graphic descriptions it's written almost as reportage, the acts and images speaking for themselves. It's also a long scene, uncomfortably long, the type of scene that, were it shown in a film, the urge to look away at some point would be overwhelming. It's an awful death and the quality of the writing absolutely underlines just how awful. There's definitely no titillation here, only feelings of utter horror – exactly as it should be.

Alongside dismemberment and evisceration, head trauma features in a number of the novels. There's something particularly disturbing about head injuries over and above those to other parts of the body and its representation either in film or books always has a profound effect.

71

Ari Aster is a fan of this particular trauma, having featured it in various manifestations in both *Hereditary* and *Midsommar* and it's a motif that features in many of the films of David Lynch; *Eraserhead's* decapitation scene, the bloody wound on the Yellow Man's head in *Blue Velvet* and most notably *Wild at Heart* that features not one but two particularly violent head traumas. Anyone who has seen Cronenberg's *Scanners* remembers *that* scene more than any other and more recent notable examples include Negan's despatch of Glenn in *The Walking Dead*, Ryan Gosling's elevator stomp in *Drive,* despatch by fire extinguisher in *Irreversible* and the death of "the Librarian" in Ben Wheatley's *Kill List*[69].

Magi and Blackwood in *Cunning Folk* and Steve in *The Reddening* are decapitated – and the former contains perhaps the most disturbing head injury in all of Adam's books: Gracey's accident, but the first blunt force trauma applied to a head comes in *Apartment 16* during the aforementioned dream that Seth has of the Shafers. At one point Seth is goaded by his ghostly companion into attacking Mrs Shafer with a brass lampstand, smashing it into her head, again and again and again.

Bricks and stamping feet are the weapons of choice of Fergal in *No One Gets Out Alive,* used to crush the head of Steph's boyfriend Ryan when he finally turns up at the house on a mercy errand. The death of Ryan snuffs out the last flame of hope Steph might have had at escaping from 82 Edgehill Rd and the death of another ex-partner also has a significant effect on the fate of a character in *The Vessel.*

In this case, Jess is not a bystander, a witness to the atrocity rather she is the perpetrator. Her ex-partner's

---

[69] A particularly upsetting but effective example personally given I was sure that the camera would cut away at the last moment when the hammer swung down. But didn't.

head is crushed to a pulp by a poker wielded by her in the climax to the novel. Counterposed dramatically with Jess's daughter Izzy playing outside, this is a brutal scene but a hugely significant one as Jess unknowingly participates in a ritual, a sacrifice, which will change her life, and that of her daughter, forever.

Profondo Rosso

Splashing blood around isn't the only way in which to incorporate red into a story and, because of the associations and symbolism the colour carries, it's unsurprising that it features in the horror genre with some regularity. Whilst the colour is associated with courage and passion, it is also linked to anger and danger, sin and sexual desire. The classic representation of Satan has him dressed in red, a reflection of the flames of Hell in which he dwells.

Using red as a visual clue is prevalent in film and among the numerus examples is the red coat worn by the murderous dwarf in *Don't Look Now* – the colour used throughout the film as foreshadowing, not least in the terrifying opening in which Donald Sutherland's daughter drowns whilst wearing a coat of the same colour. M Night Shyamalan's *Sixth Sense* uses a similar approach, using red to signify when the supernatural is impinging on the real world; the jumper Cole wears at the birthday party and the balloon that drifts up the spiral staircase, the doorknob to Crowe's basement office, the tent Cole hides in. A recent example is Alex Garland's *Men* in which much of the interior of the house in which Jessie Buckley is holidaying is decorated in red; perhaps intended as a subtle indication that she is actually in Hell[70].

---

[70] Which would make it the only subtle thing in the whole film.

Red is used symbolically in horror literature too. What was good enough for Edgar Allan Poe in *The Masque of the Red Death* is certainly good enough for Stephen King. The use of the colour features in many of the latter's novels; the iconic balloon of Pennywise in *IT*, *Christine's* livery (*not* a standard, factory colour), the light inside the underground lair of Atropos in *Insomnia*, its multiple representations and interpretations in *Rose Madder* and the field of red roses surrounding the *Dark Tower*, wherein resides the Crimson King himself to name but a few.

It's no surprise then to see that Adam is maintaining this tradition and the colour red is deployed in all of his novels both overtly and subtly. It also features heavily in the cover designs of all the Ritual Limited books, resulting in striking imagery alongside the blacks and greys which complete the palette.

A discussion of the significance or otherwise of the appearances of the colour red in the novels is beyond the scope of this book, indeed could probably provide enough material for a book of its own. It is however a characteristic feature of the books, manifesting in all of them, and as such worthy of inclusion in this chapter. What follows is simply a list of the occurrences of red throughout the books – or at least the ones I managed to spot - presented in order of publication of the novels.

In *Banquet For The Damned*, Hart Miller, the anthropologist, is wearing a red shirt on his first appearance. The university dons meet in a room with ox-blood leather chairs and crimson curtains whilst Maria, who describes her night terror to Hart Miller is sleeping beneath a red duvet when the Brown Man strikes.

The golfer who discovers the flayed body on the beach is wearing a red sweater (the body itself is obviously VERY red) and the paining in the secretary Marcia's room depicts the Brown Man carrying a red sack. Red light filters through the curtains of the cottage when Dante approaches it, inside which he finds a jacket belonging to his friend Tom which has a red lining. Later, when he returns to burn the cottage down, the petrol cans he carries are red, as is the scarf he uses as a mask whilst in the final chapter, the calm after the storm, has a woman in a red coat walking along the beach, her dog playing with a red rubber ball.

The use of red in *Apartment 16* is more overt and, along with the smells of brimstone and sulphur which permeate the interior of Barrington House, paint a vivid picture of Hell manifesting within the building. Rather than the detail flourishes of *Banquet For The Damned*, (although the doors to the rooms in The Green Man, the pub above Seth lives, are red), here the structure of the building itself is affected as the Vortex takes hold, the walls of rooms and corridors alike turned red. So too the glimpsed faces of its denizens, more often than not their images reflected in mirrors.

It's red light which illuminates Hutch's dream as recounted in *The Ritual*, (a night terror in which he is accompanied by a skeletal figure with bad teeth...) and that same hue is found in the main location of *House of Small Shadows*, the appropriately named Red House. Here its colour is due to the red skylights through which it is filtered rather than from a supernatural manifestation but that doesn't detract from its symbolism. Catherine drives to her new employment in a red mini and Edith Mason's choice of animal companion (a real one, not a stuffed one) is, of course, a red setter.

A red glow emanates from many of the locations in *Last Days* and the farmhouse in Normandy has a reddy-brown outbuilding in its grounds. The door to the apartment block in which Kyle carries out his first interview (and unknowingly encounters the Blood Friends) has a red door and the thin figures who are "smeared ruddy" who infiltrate his dreams have already been discussed. Within the Temple of the Last Days itself, the Seven, the senior members of the organisation, dress in red robes and when Kyle watches the footage of the now grown dog-translocated children barking at one another and running around on all fours he sees that they're wearing red tracksuits. When he finally tracks down and confronts Chet Regal in San Diego, the body in which Sister Katherine's soul now resides, it's no surprise that the curtains of the bedroom in which he is confined are red.

Perhaps it's the red hair of her stepmother Val that tips the balance and makes Steph up sticks and leave only to find herself in rented accommodation at 82 Edgehill Rd in *No One Gets Out Alive*. The claret flows freely in the deaths of Ryan and Knacker as discussed earlier of course and there's an early subconscious tip off to readers that Steph is in for trouble when the mat in the room she first moves into is red. Later, when Knacker and Fergal lock her away having despatched Ryan, the room that is her prison cell has red skirting boards.

Oleg, in *Lost Girl*, enigmatically refers to the novel's protagonist as Red Father – possibly a reference to the red robes in which King Death himself is clad - but the red-as-the-harbinger-of-doom visual clue in this one is that it's the colour of the top his daughter is wearing when she's abducted. Upon finding the photograph of his daughter in Oleg's shrine, the Father is stimulated by "red" energy which makes him "careen like a drunkard" and long to commit violence against someone, anyone. (The Father also gives codenames to his police contacts who help him on his quest and calls one of them Scarlett

Johansson. This is because she sounds like the actress but of course that's not necessarily the actual reason...)

The red shoreline upon which a ghostly figure is seen is mentioned on the opening page of *Under A Watchful Eye* but this is more likely an accurate description of the geology of the real location the novel is set in than any hint of the supernatural. Much like Steph's stepmother in *No One Gets Out Alive*, Julie, Seb's ex-girlfriend has red hair but once more it's stretching a point to ascribe any portentous meaning to this. The sight of his mother in a red coat when he dreams of the figure scuttling four-legged across a golf course is a lot more significant however, so too the fact that it's also the colour of the chair which is located in the room in Hunter's Tor where the experimentation into astral projection and translocation took place.

And then we come to *The Reddening*.

"The past is red, the earth is red, the sky is red. Behind is red, forward is red. The queen is risen and she is red. All we children are red. Amen."

So chant the Red People as they prepare for another sacrifice. Although the word red is used as an adjective in this prayer, the central conceit of the novel applies a definite article to it, makes it a noun: The Red.

The Red is a life force that binds everything together, the equivalent to the Chinese *Qi* or the Indian *Prana*[71]; a spirituality that infiltrates all things and which has given rise to its own form of worship, one facet of which is the reddening itself, the act of sacrifice to the physical manifestation of The Red: Old Creel.

---

[71] Or The Force in the Star Wars universe.

It's little surprise then that the colour has infiltrated all of the novels thus far, and explains the seemingly prophetic vignettes in which glimpses of red faced people occur; Kyle's dream in *Last Days*, the mirror-reflected demons of *Apartment 16*.

When I first read *The Reddening*, I had a feeling that it was a culmination of everything that had gone before in Adam's novels, that somehow everything had been leading to this point and after my re-read for this project I'm even more convinced of that opinion. It may partly be the reason why this was the first novel to be published by Ritual Limited; the book was so important, a milestone in his oeuvre, that he wanted full creative control over it. It is, in my opinion, the quintessential Nevill novel.

Such is its all-pervasive nature, it's only natural that The Red abides beyond the end of events in *The Reddening* and makes appearances in the two subsequent novels.

In *Cunning Folk*, among the bad dreams experienced by the family on their first night in their new house is Fiona's in which she sits alongside a black pond[72] applying red lipstick. A later dream sequence, this time Gracey's, features a red sky below which the *clack-clack-clack* of porcine hooves ring out.

The red door on the Moots' house marks them out as wrong 'uns of course and the red flowers scattered around the throne and altar of the Sow Beneath the Earth send out a mixed message of both beauty and danger.

Finally, in *The Vessel*, the Red appears relatively briefly but significantly; as the colour of the ribbon which binds the folder containing the death certificate of Flo Gardner's daughter Charlotte and of the slippers and robe

---

[72] Possibly a nod to the lake which "gleamed like a sheet of black glass" in Blackwood's *The Wendigo*.

worn by Flo as she sits in the garden, gazing at the grove of trees within which key events in the dark history of Nerthus House have unfolded. (And continue to unfold).

Picture This

Disturbing imagery litters the pages of Adam's novels; it's a feature of his writing that he can effortlessly create vivid scenes in readers' minds, a cinematic style of writing which has reached its ultimate – if not inevitable - conclusion of his writing screenplays, albeit ones which ultimately became novels: *Cunning Folk* and *The Vessel*.

Unsurprisingly, for someone with such a keen eye for, and appreciation of, visual impact, paintings and illustrations are a common feature of his novels, the pictures serving to enhance atmosphere or, in some cases, providing narrative clues.

The most overt use of this latter device has already been mentioned: the triptych, *The Saints of Filth*, which features in *Last Days*. Here is displayed the entire story of the persecution, martyrdom and "Ascent" of Lorche and his followers, a previous incarnation of the Temple of the Last Days. Despite the painting showing events of the past, the disturbing nature of the images in display loses none of its impact with both Kyle and readers alike transposing them into more modern day events. Even more so, given the inexplicable and terrifying events which Kyle has already encountered by the time he views the painting, and the evidence he has gathered about Sister Katherine and her cult, the scenes depicted within the triptych can no longer be seen as simply fanciful imaginings of the artist Niclaes Verhulst. The inference is that this is a depiction of real events.

A huge clue as to what is happening, and is going to happen, in Nerthus House in *The Vessel* is provided by a line drawing which carer Jess finds hanging beside a huge scythe when wandering around the building at the beginning of her tenure there. The illustration depicts a haggard figure pulling a cart beside a body of dark water. A large sphere constructed of twigs and branches sits in the cart which is in turn followed by a naked woman carrying a scythe. A long, thin figure stands in the water, merging into the dark trees behind...

Anyone who Googled "Nerthus" upon seeing the name of the house and being intrigued by it [73] will identify it as a depiction of the classic scene in which the Germanic goddess is represented: a ceremonial wagon procession. Of course, as with the mural which appears behind the opening credits of Ari Aster's *Midsommar*, the picture actually illustrates events from the narrative itself, a preview of things yet to come[74].

It could be argued that the cave paintings unearthed in *The Reddening* depicting Old Creel and the white pups on the hunt serve as a prediction of what is to come but at the very least it offers evidence of the ancient nature of the evil which lurks beneath the red earth of the south west coast of England.

The after-images of the Blood Friends in *Last Days*, the residue they leave behind on the walls and ceilings of the places they visit always put me in mind of cave paintings, so too the urban graffiti of *Lost Girl*, the painted images of the red-robed and skeletal King Death that adorned walls and buildings acting as sinister territorial markers.

The latter novel also features a painting found by the Father in one of his victim's houses, that of a typically

---

[73] Yes. I did.

[74] The mural actually tells the whole plot of the film. A more subtle hint of what's in store also featured in the film is the painting of a bear which hangs above Dani's bed.

Nevillesque emaciated figure set against turbulent skies. Its title is *L'homme Devant la Mort* – "Man Before Death". Whilst serving to add to the grim atmosphere already prevalent within the scene it also ties into the narrative of the belief system of the Kings, their fixation on, and worship of, the process of death and what happens after. Another significant painting to feature in the novel is that painted by Oleg of the Father as referred to in the Nightmares and Dreamscapes section.

Other paintings previously mentioned are those of the Brown Man as featured in *Banquet For The Damned* discovered in the cottage where the modern day coven have been enacting their rituals. These paintings add atmosphere to the story in more ways than one; not only are the images they present ghastly and unsettling, the aroma which arises from them fills the cottage with a pungent miasma. Paint has not been used to create these images, rather bodily fluids, the hideous odour arising from them as they degenerate upon the canvasses.

The fact that such extreme measures have been used in the creation of these images suggests that the "paintings" themselves are more than just representations, are in fact part of the rituals performed, have a power in themselves. This idea is taken to its most extreme in *Apartment 16*.

Art runs through this novel like blood through a body; one of the joint protagonists Seth is an artist as is the villain of the piece, erstwhile resident of Barrington House Felix Hessen. From the sketches of corpses and dead animals Apryl discovers in her on-line research into Hessen, to the cages full of the artist's work held in the building's basement (in which ghostly figures appear), to the increasingly disturbing imagery Seth himself creates, paintings play a huge role in the narrative of this novel, acting as portals between this world and that of The Vortex, allowing entry into that terrifying world but also,

81

more disturbingly, a way out for the demons and creatures which inhabit it.

The Interconnected World

Whilst each of Adam's novels is a standalone story, they all exist within the same literary universe, proof of which is found in a number of subtle references made in the various texts.

This is a device used by many authors and spotting the references and connections to other novels often adds an extra layer of enjoyment to the reading experience. Among those who employ this technique are David Mitchell of *Cloud Atlas* and *The Bone Clocks* fame and, of course, the master of them all Stephen King whose has managed to create a parallel universe centred around Castle Rock and Derry in his version of Maine, with characters moving between novels and events occurring in one book referenced in others.

Castle Rock and Derry are fictional creations of course, as are some of the locations in Adam's books but, as King does too, real places also feature and provide links between the novels.

The Torbay region of Devon which is the location of the events which unfold in *The Reddening* is also the home of Seb in *Under A Watchful Eye* and the killing ground for the Father in *Lost Girl*. The latter also features a trip to Birmingham, the location of 82 Edgehill Rd in *No One Gets Out Alive* and the home of Dante and Tom which they leave behind when they travel to St Andrews in *Banquet For The Damned*. It's also the city where the four friends of *The Ritual* shared a house during their student days.

Given these locations are the previous and current homes of the author himself, it's unsurprising that they feature in his novels. Similarly, his experiences of working in an apartment building in London no doubt informed his use of such locations in both *Apartment 16* and *Last Days*. The most overt, and significant, link between locations however is in the two most recent novels, *Cunning Folk* and *The Vessel* which are both set in – or near in the case of the former – the village of Eadric. It's possible that the black pond which Fiona dreams of is the one which features significantly in *The Vessel*; a subtle piece of foreshadowing from one book to the next.

Given it's the first of Adam's novels, *Banquet For The Damned* can't reference any of the other books (although a few templates are established within its pages) but there's a sinister appearance of the expression *manes exite paterni* on a warning note, a phrase used in the Ancient Roman festival of Lemuria which will be familiar to anyone who receives Adam's newsletter or has a signed copy of one of his books[75].

By the time the fourth novel *Last Days* was published, there was enough of a back catalogue to allow cross referencing and such is the case with references made to two previous films made by the novel's protagonist Kyle Freeman: *Coven*, an investigation into a witch cult based in St Andrews and *Blood Frenzy* which delved into the disappearance of a group of hikers in northern Sweden.

Kyle makes an appearance in two more of the novels – albeit by reference to rather than a physical manifestation. He is also the director of the documentary film made about Steph's experiences in 82 Edgehill Rd in *No One Gets Out Alive* and, given this body of work, and the supernatural elements associated with all of them, it's

---

[75] And which appears in *The Vessel* with an appropriately feminine slant as *manes exite materni*.

little surprise that Mark Fry, a character in *Under A Watchful Eye*, suggests that he would be the perfect man to make a film about the "haunted" cottage Hunter's Tor. (A building in which one significant room contains a doll sitting on a chair that could well have been taken from the private collection of Edith Mason in *House of Small Shadows*).

The subject of Kyle's investigation in *Last Days*, the Temple of the Last Days, makes a surprising appearance in *Lost Girl*. Despite being set (at the time of writing this) thirty one years hence, the organisation still exists. What's more surprising is that it is now a benevolent force, a charity offering succour to the less fortunate. There's another link in that novel too; when the Father finds the shrine in Abergil's house, which includes a huge collage made up of photographs of death and destruction, one of the images contained within is of a corpse with its face wrapped in polythene – a direct reference to the modus operandum of Fergal and Knacker in *No One Gets Out Alive*.

The Temple of Last Days gets another mention in *Under A Watchful Eye*, this time in the Theophanic Mutations - the reference book on cults written by Mark Fry which indicates that M L Hazzard and Sister Katherine knew each other. The metafictional nature of the novel allows for some self-referential stuff too; one of the books Seb is planning to write is entitled *Yellow Teeth* – about which much has already been written here – and mention is made of a short story of Hazzard's called *Hasty For The Dark*, which, of course, is the name of the second collection of Adam's short stories to be released by Ritual Limited.

There's a tenuous link to *Banquet For The Damned* with one of Seb's dreams in which a spindly figure scuttles across a golf course. The golf course isn't St

Andrews but it's still a strong visual reference. A more direct link to previous works however is the fact that Ewan, the housemate from hell, has among his scant possessions a CD from a band called Blood Frenzy.

There are musical connections to be found in *The Reddening* too. Tony Willows, the musician who has taken over the role of Lord of the Manor and who is responsible for the reawakening of Old Creel has amongst his back catalogue a song called *Old Black Mag* and has on his wall a silver disc to acknowledge sales of his record *Thin Len and Choker Lottie* – a reference to the murderous pair who haunt the pages of *Under A Watchful Eye*.

Chapter Three

The Protagonists

For horror literature to be effective it must instil feelings of fear and dread in the reader; recreate within them the same emotions they would experience were they themselves exposed to the threats being described. Any emotions felt by readers are vicarious, the experiences belong to the characters within the book and so, in order for the horror to work, those characters must be "real" enough to allow this transference of emotion. Whether or not a character is likeable is less important than whether they are relatable, allowing readers to empathise (and sympathise) with them, to share their feelings and reactions to what is happening within the plot.

It's a fine line between writing characters who are so thinly sketched that they are little more than cardboard cut-outs, there simply to progress a plotline, and overdoing the whole thing so ending up with a caricature. If horror stories are set in the real world, and not some fantasy scenario, then the characters who inhabit that world must be real too, exhibiting the flaws and weaknesses we all do (as well as any hidden strengths the scenarios they are placed in bring out) and must react realistically to the threats they face if readers are to invest in them properly.

Making the characters real can be achieved by incorporating back story into the narrative – another fine balancing act which, if handled badly simply results in info-dumping – but most effectively by recording their thoughts and emotions on the page[76]. Another way of developing character is of course by describing their reactions to the bizarre events unfolding around them, a sure way to determine personality. As Kurt Vonnegut says in the introduction to his short story collection *Bagombo Snuff Box*:

> *"Be a sadist. No matter how sweet and innocent your leading characters, make awful things happen to them -- in order that the reader may see what they are made of."*

It's fair to say that awful things happen to the characters in Adam's novels. What is also fair to say is that they are very well written, "real" people whose journeys through the various narratives completely engage the reader. What follows is a look at the characters themselves, their relationships, motivations and their ultimate fates.

Of the eleven novels under discussion, six feature male lead protagonists and four female. *Apartment 16* has both, with honours shared between Apryl and Seth.

Only two of the novels, *Lost Girl* and *Cunning Folk* feature families, in both cases married parents with a young daughter. The responsibilities of being a father undoubtedly play into the motivations of both male protagonists, Tom in *Cunning Folk* and The Father of *Lost Girl*. The fact that the latter is unnamed throughout the book, is referred to only by that appellation, underlines the significance of that role. The tagline for the Pan paperback of the novel is "Will he kill to find her?" and it's a question that gets answered fairly quickly. The moral conundrum it poses could have been phrased less

---

[76] Although Anton Chekhov may disagree. In a letter to his brother Alexander, he wrote: "Be sure *not* to discuss your hero's state of mind. Make it clear from his actions."

specifically as "how far will he go to save her?" as that is the real crux of the book. What's most profound about The Father's journey isn't that he will kill other men, it's that he does so – and continues to do so as his quest becomes all-consuming.

Lost Girl can be read as a morality play, with The Father's police contacts and Oleg, the shaman involved in the kidnap of his daughter, taking the role of the demons who egged the protagonists of the original Tudor plays towards the dark side.

The Father is perhaps the most fascinating of all Adam's characters. His plight will certainly draw sympathy from readers who will be supportive of his quest to find his daughter. That sympathy is then tested as the acts of violence he perpetrates cast a shadow over his character and the question of how far he *will* go begins to play on readers' minds, leading them to ask themselves the same question; how far would *I* go? The moral waters are muddied further by the fact that The Father has been unfaithful to his wife, was in fact planning another act of betrayal at the moment his daughter was taken. Perhaps then, his actions are driven as much by guilt as by love. This, coupled with the danger his actions put others in – his contacts, his wife – paint a conflicting picture of his character and, as that character disintegrates even further, mirroring the devastation of the world around him, readers may well feel not sorrow but a sense that just desserts have been served.

There's a similar arc followed by the other family man Tom in *Cunning Folk*. He too embarks on a course of action that will ultimately destroy everything he loves, driven on by (at least in his mind) a desire to do the right thing for his family. Guilt undoubtedly plays its part in his motivation too; the terrible injury his daughter Gracey receives comes about as a direct result of his activities.

Tom is a graphic designer and perhaps it's his artistic temperament which plays a part in his decision making. It's a feature he shares with a number of Adam's male protagonists: Dante is a musician in *Banquet For The Damned*, Seth an artist in *Apartment 16*, Kyle Freeman a film-maker in *Last Days*, and Seb, of *Under A Watchful Eye*, is an author.

That artistic temperament is most profoundly seen in Seth and it's his skill as an artist that allows the connection between himself and Felix Hessen to be made. Seth in effect becomes a portal for the occultist and his transformation throughout the course of the novel is the equivalent of a possession. Seth is single and apparently friendless so there is no one to mourn him come the end of the book as he becomes the only one of Adam's protagonists not to be still standing (in this plane of existence at least) come the final page.

Of the remaining four male lead characters, it's only Seb in *Under A Watchful Eye* that is in a relationship. But, as is so often the case in Adam's novels, that relationship falters and breaks, in this instance courtesy of the arrival of the malodorous and psychotic Ewan. Seb's cry for help to his girlfriend Becky is rebutted, her own experiences after having come within the orbit of Ewan enough to make her re-evaluate her romantic connection to Seb.

Whilst Seb's arc is perhaps less dramatic than that of Seth, they both follow a downward trajectory as forces greater than themselves slowly destroy them in order to further their own ends. This "dismantling" of male characters is a recurring theme in Adam's novels; at one point in *Lost Girl* The Father wonders

...why men were so poorly built to withstand suffering...

a supposition which finds much supporting evidence in the events of *The Ritual*. Of the four friends who venture into the dark Scandinavian forest, it's only Luke who survives until the end but even in so doing is left, literally, naked, bloody and bruised.

Adam has described the group of four friends as representative of what he calls "post-historical" men[77], part of a generation which has lived outside the epochal and visceral events of the last centuries, events which would have had character-defining impacts on them. A huge element of the novel is the way in which these men – with no experience of dealing with major hardship – react when confronted with the most primal of dangers, hunted as prey in a foreign wilderness. In truth, with the possible exception of Luke himself, (although he is prone to the odd bout of self-pity), they're all pretty awful people, seemingly unable to take any responsibility for themselves and always finding someone else to blame (usually their wives). It's little wonder that they fare so badly and it's hard not to draw the conclusion that the novel is an attack on toxic masculinity, the self-professed alpha males laid low by a force of nature that is very much female.

The book has much to say about friendship too; in particular the competitive kind of friendship that develops in some groups of men[78]. A friendship formed at university has waned over the years, at least in the eyes of Luke. An outsider by nature anyway, he regards himself as a failure in comparison to his friends whose careers have been hugely successful and, as events take a turn for the worse, the underlying tensions which have always

---

[77] Interview with Adam Nevill, author of The Ritual (2011) : Revenant (revenantjournal.com)

[78] Not exclusively of course, and certainly not *all* men.

been bubbling beneath the surface of the friendship come to the fore.

Ironically, the animosity directed towards him by Dom and Phil in particular is not because they think he is an underachiever, rather because they envy his independence, their own marriages and careers having failed[79].

There's a precursor to this concept of a friendship sitting uneasily above deep tensions in that of Dante and Tom in *Banquet For The Damned*. The two men are different in character, Tom much more the outgoing, Jack-the-lad in comparison to the more reserved and thoughtful Dante but it's the fact that Tom began a relationship with Dante's ex Imogen that provides the foundation of the resentment between them – a situation made worse by Tom leaving her to come to St Andrews with Dante.

The reality of their friendship is nicely summed up by Imogen herself when Dante phones her after Tom goes missing. Angry at her own abandonment by Tom she gives full vent to her feelings.

> *"Your friendship was always unhealthy. It's no surprise he left you. All that coercion has finally backfired..."*

Words that put a dark slant on the relationship, an implication that Tom was using Dante all along. It's perhaps not so much a friendship as a mutual dependence that keeps the men together, the bond between them strong enough to weather, and overcome, the differences between them. Strong enough that, despite the anger

---

[79] The reasons for this animosity are very different – and a lot more dramatic- in the film of course. Sometimes changes made to authors' original visions can be detrimental but that's certainly not the case here.

Dante feels for Tom he still puts his own life in danger to search for him after he goes missing.

Performing together in a band of course kept the two men close and the same situation applies to Kyle and Dan in *Last Days*, the latter providing the sound recording for the documentary films the pair make. There's no hint of any underlying tension in this friendship, the two come across as genuine mates who happen to share a passion for film making. Of the two, however, it's Kyle who is the more driven, persisting in continuing with their investigation into the Temple of the Last Days even when the threat from the Blood Friends becomes overwhelming. It says much about the nature of their friendship – and about the character of Kyle himself – that even when Dan is attacked by the monsters Kyle continues on alone. There's no sense of Kyle's motivation being revenge for the attack on his friend however – his pursuit continues because that's what he wants to do.

A friendship of sorts develops between the two female leads in *The Reddening*, Katrine and Helene who are drawn together by the activities, past and present, of the Red People. Another connection between them is their relationship history; Helene is a single mother, her daughter Valda the product of a short liaison with a former boyfriend Mitch who now lives in Australia and has nothing to do with his child. Katrine's ex-husband is an even weaker man, the toxic Graham, a selfish, manipulative and passive aggressive individual whose infidelity led to an STD which, when passed onto Katrine, made her infertile. In an "out of the frying pan into the fire" type scenario, Katrine is now in a relationship with Steve whose higher social class makes him patronise and look down on her.

Steve, of course, comes to a horrible end and it's tempting to think that there's an element of poetic justice being meted out by Adam here as it's a fate shared by all of the "bad" men who appear in his novels.

The fates of Hutch, Dom and Phil have already been discussed but this divine retribution is also brought down onto the heads of Tony, the violent ex of Jess in *The Vessel* and Mike, the former boyfriend of Catherine in *House of Small Shadows*, a man who left her not once, but twice – the second time following Catherine's miscarriage.

There's a similar grisly fate for Ryan, the ex-boyfriend of Steph, in *No One Gets Out Alive*. In this case it's Steph who has left Ryan, realising that his over-protective personality was one she could no longer live with. It's a cruel twist of fate that it's the desperation of the situation she finds herself in that brings him to her "rescue", the money she needs to escape the horrors of 82 Edgehill Rd in his pocket; his arrival at the building bringing him into the world of Knacker and Fergal and leading to his violent death.

Steph's decision to leave Ryan indicates a strength of character that is a major component of why she is able to survive the horrors thrown at her during her time at 82 Edgehill Rd. In fact, it's generally the case that the female protagonists of Adam's novels tend to reach the ends of the books in better shape than the male ones[80]. This is most notable in *Apartment 16* in which the disintegration of character is all Seth's whilst Apryl, who is exposed to the same terrors, remains relatively unscathed.

It's the authenticity of these characters, with all their flaws and weaknesses, that makes the horrors they are pitted against all the more terrifying. These are "ordinary"

---

[80] A notable exception being Kat in *The Reddening* who ends the book institutionalised.

people faced with extraordinary threats and, because they are such well-formed creations, readers are able to identify with them and establish that vicarious link; the horrors they endure provide a shared experience.

One of the reasons given for why people enjoy horror is this vicarious element – experiencing terror and fear from a safe distance and under no actual threat to oneself. The question of what would I do? under the same circumstances is one that often occurs. Horror movies will elicit cries of "don't go in there!" or "get out now!" and many other variations on the theme. As external observers we like to think that we would never be so stupid as to get into that kind of situation.

And yet the characters in Adam's novels *do* get into those types of situation, something that happens deliberately or purely by chance; the "wrong place at the wrong time" scenario.

That is definitely the case in *The Ritual* in which the four friends literally stray off the beaten track and get lost in the dense forest. It's the "weak" men of the group, Dom and Phil, who force the decision to divert from the planned route, their lack of fitness – and the damage done to their bodies as a result – making a shortcut necessary, a shortcut that takes them straight into Moder's realm. The fact that they are "roughing it", going on a hiking/camping expedition in the first place is because of Luke's financial situation, something which only adds to the resentment Dom and Phil feel towards him.

Another victim of stumbling unwittingly into danger is Steph in *No One Gets Out Alive*. It's circumstances which dictate that she takes up residence in 82 Edgehill Rd, a place that, given the choice, she wouldn't touch with a bargepole. Indeed, a great deal of the book's tension derives from her fruitless attempts to break free and leave and it's to Adam's credit that the reasons he comes up with for Steph staying as long as she does are entirely credible.

When Tom and Fiona move into their new home on the outskirts of the village of Eadric they of course have no idea of what lies in store for them courtesy of the cunning folk who are their neighbours and it's the death of her elderly aunt which brings Apryl all the way from America to the horrors of Barrington House. Again, it's circumstance and coincidence which brings all of these characters into contact with the supernatural threats which reside in those locations.

Whereas the four friends in *The Ritual* – and Luke in particular – and Steph in *No One Gets Out Alive* spend the course of the books simply fighting to survive, the situation in which the others find themselves prompts them into action; Apryl undertakes an investigation into Felix Hessen and Tom begins his war of attrition with the Moots, placing himself and his family in even greater danger. The same can be said of Helene and Kat in *The Reddening*, particularly the latter who, having found herself in a dangerous situation continues her investigation into the events around Divilmouth.

The two protagonists who are most proactive in the novels are The Father of *Lost Girl* and Kyle Freeman in *Last Days*. Neither have stumbled into their particular scenarios of horror; the Father is responding to a terrible act committed against his family whilst Kyle is employed to undertake his investigations into Sister Katherine's activities. Even as the horrors unfold and increase around them they continue along the path of their chosen quests despite the damage and harm it does both to themselves but also the people – friends and family – around them.

In the remaining four novels, there's a definite sense that the protagonists have been chosen, by forces beyond the normal, to participate in the events which unfold. This notion of unknowingly being part of a bigger picture is most overt in *House of Small Shadows*. Catherine is employed in the first instance to make a valuation of the contents of the Red House but in reality her history and fate have been intertwined with that of the building, and its residents, since her childhood and she is in fact fulfilling her destiny by entering the employ of Edith Mason.

It's a similar scenario in *The Vessel* with Jess being employed to care for Flo Gardner in Nerthus House. There's no prior history with the location as was the case in *House of Small Shadows* but, given the way the narrative plays out, the fact that Jess has a young daughter is undoubtedly a major factor in the decision to employ her[81].

Whilst it's her profession and family situation that makes Jess the perfect "pick" in *The Vessel*, it's previous relationships which lead to the protagonists of the remaining two novels being chosen to meet their destinies.

In *Banquet For The Damned*, Dante already has a relationship of sorts with Eliot Coldwell, the author of the book which gives the novel its name. Inspired by the book, Dante composed the album which shares its name and struck up a correspondence with the academic, that connection facilitating Coldwell's request for Dante to come to St Andrews and assist him in his research. Coldwell's motives are of course a lot more sinister; Dante is being used as a way out of the horrors he has unleashed as a result of his dabbling in arcane rituals.

Another contact made in the past which brings about horrendous events in the present is that made between Seb

---

[81] The endings of both of these books gave me a definite "July Ball 1921 photograph at the end of Kubrick's *The Shining*" vibe.

and Ewan in *Under A Watchful Eye*. Their first encounter during university days was bad enough for Seb but the return of his malodorous and slovenly friend is even worse. Seb is an innocent victim, drawn into the horrors emanating from Hunter's Tor by the actions and decisions of someone else.

Ironically, having spent most of the first half of the book wishing for Ewan to go, it's when he finally does, and his subsequent death alone in a B&B, that provides the catalyst for Seb to pursue the leads and evidence that have been left behind for him. Thus Seb becomes yet another character seemingly motivated by guilt, that emotion taking him into the darkness that pervades the world of M L Hazzard and his acolytes.

What's in a Name?

M any authors will tell you that choosing names for their characters is one of the hardest things about writing - there are even random name generators available on the internet for those who find it too much of a struggle. There are a number of approaches to coming up with them, ranging from simply finding one that "sounds right" to referencing other characters (or actual people) by way of homage to finding names with some significance to the story being told. In most cases, especially for authors with a large back catalogue it will be a combination of all these approaches.

Stephen King's Roland Deschain takes his name from *Childe Roland to the Dark Tower Came*, the poem by Robert Browning which inspired his *Dark Tower* series of books whilst John Coffey, the tragic hero of *The Green Mile* shares his initials with someone else who was executed (sacrificed even) despite being innocent. Dolores

97

Claiborne's first name is derived from *dolor*, a word for pain, suffering and sorrow which fits her character very nicely whilst the religious allusions of the Creeds (whose cat is called Church) are hard to ignore in *Pet Sematary*, a novel which is very much a meditation on death and what comes after. Randall Flagg, so legend has it, was inspired by a company name the author saw on the side of a truck...[82]

There's some debate as to where the name James Bond came from, he was either an ornithologist living in the Caribbean whose book Ian Fleming had read or an agent Fleming had worked alongside during his time in Naval Intelligence. Whichever, the punchy pair of single syllable names was something Clive Cussler admitted to copying when naming his recurring hero Dirk Pitt.

Of course sometimes it's just as easy to use the name of someone famous and apply it to your character, Hieronymous (Harry) Bosch in Michael Connelly's novels and Charlie Parker in John Connolly's crime/supernatural series.

Whilst the derivations of some of Adam's characters' names are obvious, others require a bit more digging. Some, of course, have no significance attached to them and it behoves me at this point to say that the theories I have concocted for the choice of some of the names, and which are listed here, are mine and mine alone and – quite possibly in many of the cases – completely wrong.

The first of Adam's novels, *Banquet For The Damned*, contains the highest number of referential names of them all. The name of the book's protagonist, Dante Shaw, is even remarked upon as being "appropriate" in the novel itself, by Eliot Coldwell's secretary Janice when he first

---

[82] And it's not hard to work out where Christopher Fowler's detective duo of Bryant and May got their monikers.

introduces himself. The reference is of course to Dante Alighieri whose most famous work *The Divine Comedy* (specifically Part One of the poem: *Inferno*) describes a journey through Hell, a trip Dante Shaw is about to embark upon himself.

There's a similarity between Coldwell and Karswell of course, the latter being the alchemist and occultist who appears in the M R James story *Casting the Runes*.[83] That James connection is also apparent in the name of the librarian character, Rhodes Hodgson; his Christian name taken from the R of M R James and his surname shared with that other purveyor of fantastic fiction William Hope Hodgson

It's never specified whether Beth, the name of the partner to Eliot Coldwell and the vessel for the reincarnated spirit of a medieval witch, is a shortened version of Elizabeth, Elsbeth, Bethan or Bethany. Being Scottish, it's most likely the second of those options but if it is Bethany then she shares a name with the hometown of Lazarus, the biblical figure who was raised from the dead and so that naturally makes it my favoured option.

There's a passing nod to another author of weird fiction in the book's opening chapter in which the Brown Man attacks a student called Walter. The unfortunate young man meets his demise in the sea so, if one were

---

[83] The film adaptation is *Night of the Demon*, a personal favourite of mine (and of so many others old enough to have seen it on BBC2's double bill of horror films which were shown in the 80s). In an interesting parallel, the main character in the film is changed from the British researcher Edward Dunning to a visiting American psychologist Dr John Holden. *Banquet For The Damned* has its own visiting American psychologist of course, Hart Miller.

showing a bit of gallic flair, it would be perfectly reasonable to call him Walter *de la mer*.[84]

Even with a powerful search engine and a willingness to see significance in the most tenuous of links it was hard to find evidence of any influences in the selection of names for the characters in *Apartment 16*.

That said, it could be that Seth, the joint-protagonist is named after the incorporeal spirit who dictated his thoughts to psychic and medium Jane Roberts from which *The Seth Material*, a book which provided a cornerstone of New Age philosophy, was published. Roberts maintained that "Seth" spoke to her from a separate plane of existence – which is precisely where the Seth of the novel ends up come the narrative's conclusion.

The names chosen by the three members of Blood Frenzy, Loki, Fenris and Surtr in *The Ritual* are of course derived from Norse Mythology but it's Luke whose name carries some potentially significant connotations. Outside the world of music, one of the most well-known groups of four men are the evangelists, responsible for the gospels which make up the New Testament of the bible. Like the characters in *The Ritual*, this group of four had among them a Luke who is now associated within the church with themes of sacrifice. All four evangelists have icons which are used to represent them in religious art; Matthew is an angel, Mark a winged lion, John an eagle whilst Luke is represented by an ox – a large animal with horns and cloven hooves.

House of Small Shadows features the first of Adam's Catherines, the name appearing (as Katherine) in *Last Days* and (as Katrine) in *The Reddening*. It's obviously a favourite name of the author, as it was of Henry VIII who

---

[84] De la Mare translates as "of the pond", a much less impressive body of water.

managed to marry three Catherines, annulling his marriage to one, executing another and being outlived by the third. Catherine Howard was the unfortunate victim of the executioner's axe but it's her surname, as well as her Christian name that she shares with the protagonist of *House of Small Shadows*.

Other than the name, there's nothing that really links the historical and fictional women so it's possibly another Catherine who provided the impetus to choose this particular name. Saint Catherine – specifically Catherine of Alexandria and not one of the other nine Saint Catherines.

It's the manner of her death that potentially makes her the choice of influence, in particular the torture she suffered before her beheading. Attempts were made to "break her on the wheel", a horrifying process in which the victims were strapped to a wheel and slowly dismembered[85]. Whilst this does not happen to Catherine herself in the book, it *is* the fate of Henry Stader, whose martyrdom is recreated in the cruelty play watched by her.

Stader is the source of the malign forces which surround the Red House and its environs but his legacy is maintained by Edith Mason and the now deceased M H Mason. This use of initials rather than a Christian name is possibly a homage to the previously mentioned M R James who is undoubtedly a major influence on Adam's work. The first initial is shared of course and it's a template that is used in a later book, for another villain, M L Hazzard in *Under A Watchful Eye*.

The independent nature of his profession and life in general is nicely summarised in Kyle Freeman's surname in *Last Days*. It's a nice touch that the organisation which employs him to investigate Sister Katherine is called

---

[85] And from which Catherine Wheel fireworks get their name.

Revelation Films – an entirely appropriate name for a business which creates documentaries but it's the biblical references the name carries that most readers will pick up on. The owner of the company is Maximillian Solomon and a little digging into the life and times of the most famous Solomon of all reveals that it wasn't just his wisdom that he was renowned for. The ancient king of Israel also makes an appearance in the *Gnostic Apocalypse of Adam*[86], in charge of a horde of demons who he despatches to chase down a virgin who has fled from him. Indeed, in his very own *Testament of Solomon*, he details his power over demons and his ability to control them. It's a nice twist then that the Max Solomon of *Last Days* is in a reverse scenario, as a former member of the Temple of the Last Days it's he who is being hunted down by demons; the Blood Friends, his employment of Kyle his only way of escaping their clutches.

The significance of Steph's name change to Amber Hare after she escapes 82 Edgehill Rd in *No One Gets Our Alive* has already been discussed in the Animal Magic section and, given she spends the majority of the book confined to a small room, her original surname of Booth seems entirely appropriate.

The Irish heritage of Fergal Donegal is more than apparent in his name as is the case for his cousin Knacker McGuire. Knackers are the people whose job it is to clear away the carcasses of animals then to render them down into by-products like fat and tallow. In the past they were also employed as court executioners. As nicknames go, it's a perfect one for the grubby landlord given the horrific crimes that are perpetrated within the apartment

---

[86] In which Adam (not *that* Adam) addresses his third son Seth (not *that* Seth).

block, the terrible murders and subsequent disposal of evidence they require.

It's hugely significant that the main character in *Lost Girl* is un-named, is referred to throughout simply as The Father, the emphasis firmly placed on *what* he is rather than *who* he is. By removing his individuality he becomes almost a generic representation of what a parent is and the moral and ethical dilemmas he has to face, the peril he has to place himself in, are placed in the context of that specific familial role rather than being examinations of his own character alone.

M L Hazzard in *Under A Watchful Eye* is another example of the double initial template mentioned earlier but as well as giving a nod to M R James, it's possible that one of the aliases he is discovered to have used during his varied career could be another authorial reference; the surname of the pseudonymous Magnus Ackerman certainly bears a similarity to Aickman, although Forrest J Ackerman, the American science fiction editor, is another possibility.

There are a couple of possible explanations behind the choice of the name Ewan for the entropic force who enters and disrupts the peaceful life of Seb. One possible meaning of the name in Celtic languages is "yew tree" – a tree with folkloric connections to immortality and resurrection which fits nicely into the notion of the transference of the soul which is a theme of the book.

Ewan is also a Latin word which means Bacchus – the god of, among many other things, insanity and ritual madness. He is associated with frenzied orgies which free his followers from self-conscious fear and oppression, is the embodiment of hedonism and disorder.

It's possible that this underlying theme of freeing the soul is also reflected in the character name of Mark Fry, researcher and author of the *Theophanic Mutations* who

Seb turns to for help when trying to uncover the truth behind what happened at Hunter's Tor. Could it be that the name is a phonetic play on the German *macht frei* which translates as "make free"? (Most notoriously used in "*arbeit macht frei*" – "work makes you free", the motto which adorned the main gates into Auschwitz). Given the aims of M L Hazzard are to free the soul from the body, it certainly seems apt.

The fictional location of Divilmouth which features in *The Reddening* provides a (not so) subtle hint at what is to come, and what has come to pass, within its environs but with respect to the character names there's little to suggest any intricate and devious motivation for their choice[87].

There's certainly a Gallic feel to both Katrine and Helene (and a definite Germanic influence on Helene's daughter's chosen name of Valda) but, other than Katrine being another variation on Catherine it's hard to find any connections to mythology, folklore or the themes of the book to find any significance to the names[88].

There's perhaps something to be read into the choice of Willows as the surname of the book's antagonist. *The Willows* is a story by Algernon Blackwood, an undoubted influence on Adam's writing, which features the titular trees exhibiting the type of behaviour ancient folklore believes them capable of: uprooting themselves to chase intruders. (As an aside, its branches are regarded as useful tools for warding off evil spirits and, perhaps most significantly of all, are used to make wicker, the material of choice for containment during ritual sacrifice).

The name references are much more overt in *Cunning Folk*. The Moots are Magi, originally the name of

---

[87] Even for someone who came up with the *macht frei* theory.

[88] That said… Katrine is shortened to Kat throughout the book. Old Creel is canine and, as anyone who has seen a Tom & Jerry cartoon knows, dogs and cats are mortal enemies.

Zoroastrian priests but later a general term for practitioners of magic and Medea, named after the priestess of Hecate in Greek mythology.

The name of Tom and Fiona's daughter Gracey brings with it connotations of charm, innocence and all-round niceness – characteristics that make the terrible accident she has seem all the more dreadful.

Cunning Folk is the most comedic of Adam's novels and there's a nice in-joke in the naming of the healer and expert in magic whose services Tom employs: Blackwood. He is only ever referred to by his surname in the novel but the business card he gives Tom displays the initial A which means that it might just be Algernon.

The village of Eadric is the shared location of both *Cunning Folk* and the follow-up novel *The Vessel*. A search on that slightly odd sounding name brings up quite a few hits, including a king of Kent who reigned between 685 and 686. A more likely inspiration however is Eadric the Wild, an Anglo-Saxon resistance fighter who fought against the Norman invaders. Such was his reputation that he found himself incorporated into stories of the Wild Hunt, the ghostly riders of Northern European folklore whose appearance signals some catastrophe to come.

Within Eadric is Nerthus House in which the events of *The Vessel* unfold. Nerthus is a goddess of German paganism and is associated with, and usually depicted in, a ceremonial wagon procession. This, of course, has a direct link to the narrative of the novel which features its own deadly procession and earth deity[89].

---

[89] Indeed, much in the same way as the aforementioned tapestry which features in the opening titles of Ari Aster's Midsommar which tells the whole story of the film to come, there's a scene early in the book in which Jess finds an illustration depicting the evens of the procession in the grounds around the house.

In another author reference as subtle as A Blackwood in *Cunning Folk*, Jess's surname is McMachen, the Mc giving a Caledonian spin to the Cambrian Machen of Arthur fame. And Flo Gardner herself drops a few hints as to her character with her name. Flo is short for Florence, a name which means "I blossom" or "I flourish" – both of which appropriately describe the change in Flo once Jess's daughter Izzy arrives in the house. She is – or was – a gardener too but there's also hints in that surname towards her association with the earth deity she, and the other residents of Eadric, worship and pay tribute to.

Chapter Four

Social Commentary

Much as the characters in Adam's novels are "real" people, so the world in which he places them is authentic too. With the exception of *Lost Girl*, all of the books are set in the present day and as such, reflect the environment and societies in which the narratives take place.

Whilst none of the books are overtly political, a seam of social commentary runs through them all and in a number of cases it's the personal situations of the characters which guides their motivations and actions.

Banquet For The Damned was originally published in 2004 by PS publishing and then by Virgin Books in 2008 but 2010 marked the beginning of the run of annual releases that has continued (mostly) until the present day. That same year saw the election of the Conservative-led coalition government and the implementation of its austerity programme which, despite the Prime Minister's oft-repeated claims that "we're all in this together", [90]impacted hugely on those at the lower end of the economic spectrum whilst leaving the better off relatively unscathed. In 2010 there were estimated to be 61,000 people using food banks in the UK, present day figures are in the region of 2,000,000. (Many, if not all, of these are made up of the 12,000,000 people currently living in poverty, 3,000,000 of whom are children).

The sheer awfulness of simply existing for so many people is referenced in the first book of the run beginning

---

[90] A phrase which appears on posters issued by the Ministry of Information in Terry Gilliam's *Brazil*.

in 2010, *Apartment 16*. Protagonist Seth is a victim of the poverty trap, lodging in a dingy room above a pub (with its own coterie of ghosts and history of atrocity) and pays rent – when he can – by undertaking the graveyard shift at Barrington House as nightwatchman. A summation of the conditions he lives in, and those of many parts of the country (and London specifically given it's the location of the novel) comes late on in the book when co-protagonist Apryl is approached by a beggar. She has no change and tries to move on, eliciting a sigh from the man followed by a profanity.

It wasn't directed at her, but at the cold, relentless misery of his life. At the dirty streets, the grey ugly council housing, the bent iron railings and the dying black grass...
The people here didn't need to dream of such terrible things. They lived among them.

Much is made of the fact that Tom and Fiona are escaping the horrors of renting in *Cunning Folk*, finally getting a foot on the property ladder, but it's Steph in *No One Gets Out Alive* who truly finds herself in the hell of low cost rented accommodation.

It's her lack of money that forces her into taking a room at 82 Edgehill Rd of course and also what keeps her there when she really wants to leave with every fibre of her being. It's this lack of choices that poverty brings which is one of its most debilitating features; opportunities to make things better simply aren't there.

On the flip side of the coin are the rich and those who inhabit the pages of Adam's novels are, to a person, awful. The residents of Barrington House in *Apartment 16* are among the worst, mega-rich and bereft of any sympathetic attributes. It's the effects of Seth's possession by Felix Essen which renders them genuinely monstrous of course but their personalities and characteristics in reality are far from appealing; believing themselves superior to everyone else, ordering around the staff in true master/servant style with their "affected accents" and "vulgar furnishings". A typical request from Mr Glock, the middle-aged Swiss playboy whom Seth counts among the worst of the residents little more than a barked "do it now" command.

Another rich person with an air of superiority is Edith Mason in *House of Small Shadows*, her existence in the Red House a throwback to Victorian times, reliant on the ministrations of her maid Maude. It's a way of life she has been accustomed to since birth and one she is absolutely willing to kill for in order to preserve.

The narrative of *Lost Girl* suggests that this divide between rich and poor is not only still present thirty years hence but is actually worse. Safely hidden away in gated communities with security guards to protect them, they thrive in a world which is decaying around them, their wealth not only buying them their safety but also human lives; it is the hugely wealthy Karen Perucchi who has financed the kidnap of the Father's daughter – buying a child, because she can.

There's retribution of course, for Karen and her partner Richard, violent and bloody, proof that no amount of money in the world is protection against a wronged father with a gun and a deranged Russian shaman with a scythe. There's also a hint of karma in play in *The Ritual* too, Dom and Phil are a bank marketing director and property developer respectively and both come to very nasty ends, in contrast to the "dreamer and loser" who is Luke[91].

Personal wealth, and earnings, are a blunt instrument to determine a person's class, (class itself being an entirely arbitrary distinction of course). This misplaced sense of superiority those with more money bestow upon themselves is displayed by a number of characters in the novels; Tom's first explanation for the Moots' aggressive behaviour towards him and his family in *Cunning Folk* is that it is class warfare in action, the obviously well-to-do middle class neighbours resentful of the intrusion of "people who rent" into their cosy existence; Steve, the ill-fated boyfriend of Kat in *The Reddening* is described as being from a higher social class, a situation which manifests in patronising behaviour towards her and then there's Ewan, the flatmate from hell who impacts on Seb's quiet existence in *Under A Watchful Eye*. He's upper class and as a result entitled and arrogant, looking down on Seb – a working class man "made good" – even accusing him of "Putting on a posh voice" when he writes.

The existence of a class system by its very nature excludes the possibility of a functioning society. Allocating individuals into categories stresses their differences from one another not their common ground and shared ideals. It's not precisely clear when any real attempts at maintaining a society began to break down although the then Prime Minister of the UK Margaret Thatcher's 1987[92] quote of "there's no such thing as society" should maybe regarded less as an observation than a mission statement given her championing of liberal

---

[91] Although it's a theory that's a little undermined by the fact that both men are on their uppers, their marriages and businesses both failing.

[92] Coincidentally the same year as Gordon Gekko proclaimed "greed is good!" in Oliver Stone's *Wall Street*.

market economies which involved selling off most of the nation's public assets into private ownership and encouraging the "every man for himself" philosophy.

This loss of community spirit and lack of people looking out for one another is an issue at the heart of *Cunning Folk*, a topic which Adam eloquently discusses in his afterword to the novel, a shift from the sharing and caring attitude that used to be the norm to a more self-centred "this is mine" philosophy where everyone else is regarded as a threat, not to be trusted.

Attitudes, of course, which are regarded as gold dust by politicians who follow the "divide and conquer" methodology, whipping up hatred of the "other" both as a way to distract from their own shortcomings and to whip up support from the easily influenced.

The shift towards populism has been gaining momentum over the last few decades, dragging along with it the evil twin of patriotism, nationalism. Among the many disturbing images to be found in *The Reddening* are those on display during a scene set in a fete in the town of Redhill. Merchandise bearing the image of Old Creel is on sale, much of it depicting the monster swathed in union flags, with some of the representations having it wiping its clawed feet – and worse – on the EU flag.

The Red People are a cult of course, and this scene provides a lovely piece of allegory for the 52% of the 70% of the voting population who decided to impose huge economic sanctions on the country by leaving the world's biggest single market, mainly as a way of protecting themselves from the "other".[93]

The "media" played a huge part in the dissemination of propaganda leading up to that particular vote and

---

[93] Although not mentioned in the book (given it was published in 2011) Hutch says "say Brexit" when taking a group selfie in the film version of *The Ritual*. In an ironic way…

continue to do so now, marking a shift – in newspapers at least – away from simply reporting stories, bringing people the news to being mouthpieces for the opinionated. Quite how much impact this has is open to discussion; people tend to buy newspapers which reflect their own opinions anyway, whichever side of the political divide they lie on.

"Lie" being the operative word of course. Embellishment of stories by newspapers is nothing new but it's often the case that manipulation of the facts and the selective use of them to present a manufactured picture of an individual can have devastating consequences.

The horrors of press intrusion and the engineering of narratives is reflected in the treatment of Steph/Amber when she finally escapes the nightmare of 82 Edgehill Rd in *No One Gets Out Alive*. Eager to sensationalise the story of her ordeal, her status as a victim soon gets lost in the hyperbole eventually leading to her being branded as a sex worker despite resisting the efforts of Knacker and Fergal to make her become one and then, in one particularly lurid headline, a "castratrix".

This *interpretation* of her by the press – "for its own entertainment" - is what leads her into an emotional breakdown and forces her into hiding, more so even than the events which took place in Birmingham.

There is an argument that this type of "journalism" treats the readers as fools, serving up salacious gossip as truth; "dumbing down" if you will. It's a criticism that can be levelled at the (real) entertainment media too with the huge range of outlets and viewing platforms giving rise to such a quantity of material that quality has to diminish inversely.

In a world where watching someone open a box, or observe someone listening to a song is regarded as entertainment it's difficult to disagree with the idea. It's certainly a sentiment Kyle Freeman espouses in *Last Days*, in particular the desire for fame at any cost that seems to drive so many people, desperate to be "famous for being famous", one that leads him to rant at his partner Dan:

> *"Big Brother... I'm a twattish celebrity. Strictly Come dumb-fuck Dancing. On ice!... Is this the best we can do? After millions of years of evolution, we start stupid cults of celebrity and feed the egos of maniacs until they take our money, fuck us in the arse, and then cut our throats."*

This multi-faceted disintegration of society of course leads inevitably to the verging-on-dystopian world which is presented in *Lost Girl*. Set almost forty years ahead of its time of writing (and thirty years ahead of this book), it's a terrifying glimpse at what awaits the world if the status quo of the present is allowed to continue.

Whilst it may go a little easy on the government of the future – who come across as relatively benign, willing to accept refugees into the country and with the far right relegated to the fringes – it proved unerringly correct in its prediction of an outbreak of a pandemic caused by a coronavirus originating from a wet market in China.

That was a prediction based on established data and projections of course[94] just as the huge environmental catastrophe which forms the backdrop of the novel was. Whilst this is the most overt representation of the horrors of climate change, there have been more subtle references to environmental concerns in other of Adam's books.

Earth deities in one form or another appear in *No One Gets Out Alive* (Black Maggie), *Cunning Folk* (The Sow

---

[94] Though still *hugely* impressive.

Beneath the Earth) and *The Vessel* (the un-named creature that dwells in the black pond). It's in *The Ritual* and *The Reddening* however, that the allegorical use of monsters is its most potent; both novels feature mankind encroaching into their respective domains and unleashing the horrors that dwell therein upon themselves. The monsters are "real" of course, within the universe Adam has created, but their use as metaphors in this world cannot be underestimated; man tampers with nature, nature fights – or bites - back.

Chapter Five

Form, Style and Voice

The influence of the authors of the classic era of ghost stories – James, De la Mare, Blackwood et al – on his own writing has been freely acknowledged by Adam himself and the traditional, educated voices of these authors is very much reflected in his own writing style. Literary, and at times poetic, his prose is a delight to read, creating vivid images in readers' minds, painting a backdrop against which the narratives can unfold.

There's a danger of course of allowing a desire to recreate this classical style of writing to tip over into pastiche, something he admits was the case for his short story *The Original Occupant* which appeared in the short story collection *Some Will Not Sleep*[95]. That one "indiscretion" aside however, the perfect balance between literary prose and plot-driven narratives is something he has mastered, allowing the best of both worlds when reading one of his novels; beautifully constructed prose and engaging plots.

It's a style that has been present since his first novel, *Banquet For The Damned* and examples of this classical voice are found throughout.

---

[95] The pastiche was so accurate that, when I first read the story I assumed it was set in the 1920s or earlier and was thus a little taken aback when a helicopter appeared.

They form a triangle, divided by heavy silence in a room made red by the ox-blood leather of the furniture they sit upon, and by the crimson velvet curtains that droop, half closed, over large windows facing inland. Smoke from a cigarette hangs in skeins above their heads, where a myriad of dust particles falls through a beam of sunlight…

And:

Illumined by something more than the first stars and the moon, the sky remains bright. It's as if the night is unwilling to release the sun completely after it has baked the ground hard and warmed the stones of St Andrews throughout the long day.

The novel is written in present tense, a technique which lends a sense of immediacy to proceedings and, arguably, involves the readers more as active participants in the story, uncovering the narrative in tandem with the characters. It's a narrative voice that was dropped for the next eight novels but which has been resurrected for the two most recent books, *Cunning Folk* and *The Vessel*.

The use of present tense in these novels reflects the fact that both were adapted from screenplays (written by Adam himself) that are both in development as actual films. Although both are adaptations, a different approach was taken in how the transformation into novels was achieved.

Cunning Folk is much more of a "tie in" novel, taking the dialogue and stage directions of the screenplay and expanding it into literary form, adding scenes for context and delving deeper into the thoughts and motivations of the characters. *The Vessel*, however, is a much more direct transfer of the screenplay into book form which eschews the potential to expand on the characters and to delve into their minds, instead relying totally on the action around them, and their reactions to it, to convey their feelings and thoughts. Exactly in the same way as a film would of course[96].

This (hugely successful) attempt to present a film in the form of a novel is reflected in the structure of the book too; the chapters are very short, each corresponding to a scene in the film and there's much intercutting between separate but concurrent pieces of action, a paragraph here, a paragraph there which certainly adds momentum and gives a truly cinematic feel to proceedings.

Whilst the book is so skilfully written that the characters are still so well formed that we care about what happens to them, it was still a bold move to lose the chance to get inside their heads the expanded format of a novel usually allows. Much of the horror in Adam's books is psychological; the characters having to deal with the supernatural and other threats they find themselves confronted with and it's a horror he conveys brilliantly.

Getting inside characters' heads allows for exploration of motivation and also lets readers see the changes in their outlook, and personalities. Most of the characters in Adam's novels have the horror thrust upon them but in *Lost Girl*, the Father actively pursues his goals, placing himself in harm's way. Despite this, he is still changed by his experiences – and not in a good way – and, in all the books, he is probably the most introspective. The degeneration of his own character mirrors that of the world around him and, during yet another confrontation with the criminal lowlifes he is hunting down on the way to finding his daughter, he is struck by the realisation of what he has become.

---

[96] Unless a voiceover is added, or huge swathes of expository dialogue.

I am nothing but a thing soaked to its skin, in clothes two years ragged, holding a gun. I am shorn, bespattered, psychopathic, bestially liberated. And I am here for you.

The whole novel is told from the Father's point of view and he appears in every chapter, every scene. The same is true for *No One Gets Out Alive* in which all of the events which unfold are seen through the eyes of Steph. This limited third person technique is hugely effective in the novel, creating a sense of claustrophobia for readers as well as Steph, trapping them in the hell of 82 Edgehill Rd alongside her, unable to break free for some, any, respite[97]. The tension created is almost unbearable.

Catherine, in *House of Small Shadows*, undergoes a similar journey to Steph and that novel too is written in limited third person, with everything experienced through the eyes of Catherine – apart from one chapter near the end which focuses on Leonard, the villain of the piece. The reason for this break from the limited perspective is to provide some exposition for readers, context for what is happening – and has happened – which would otherwise have been impossible to include unless a clunky speech was inserted a la James Bond villains explaining exactly what their plans for world domination are.

It's a technique which is also used in *Apartment 16*, again near the end of the book when the sequence of alternating chapters between Seth and Apryl is interrupted by one featuring Stephen, the head porter of Barrington House whose destiny and existence are tied into the apartment block in ways more than simply professional.

---

[97] This is Adam's longest book too, which makes the ordeal even greater.

A third outing for this technique is to be found in *The Reddening* (another novel with – for the most part – a shared limited third person narrative) in which, at the beginning of part three, the focus switches to Tony Willows and his family by way of explaining the events which occurred in the past to create the situation Kat and Helene find themselves embroiled in.

A limited third person perspective is also to be found in *Last Days*, with all the action seen through the eyes of Kyle Freeman – a man almost as driven as the Father of *Lost Girl* – and also in the second part of *The Ritual*, a move necessitated by the fact that Luke is the only one of the four friends to survive that long. With the switch in point of view, so comes a switch in the tone of the novel, something which led to comments that *The Ritual* was a "book of two halves". In one respect that's true, the horror shifts from the frantic terrors of being stalked by a monster to a more psychological form with Luke trying to make sense of the weirdness in which he now finds himself. The shift is certainly not as jarring as some critics might suggest and the transition is very well handled, Luke's horror during his confinement made all the profound by what he has already endured. There's a similar shift in *No One Gets Out Alive*, almost a reversal of the scenario in *The Ritual*; the first part of the book dealing with Steph's imprisonment, the second with her proactive attempts to end the horrors of Black Maggie.

The last limited third person narrative is that of *Under A Watchful Eye*. This, of course, is a novel which probably deserves its own chapter on form and structure, a book in which the metaphysical nature of its narrative extends and transforms into a metafictional construct that is full of knowing self-references and which is probably as much about the process of writing itself as it is a work of fiction; Ewan, whose arrival heralds the destruction of

119

Seb's mundane life can be seen as a muse of sorts (a dark muse obviously) whilst Wendy and Veronica, the acolytes of M L Hazzard who pick up where Ewan leaves off are surely a thinly veiled allusion to the types of fans who believe they know better than the authors, the type of keyboard warriors who believe that they are justified in telling creators exactly where they have gone wrong.

The final part of *Under A Watchful Eye* contains the only first person narrative to be found in any of Adam's novels[98]. It's introduction comes as a shock, a beautifully timed literary device which throws everything that has preceded it into a new light.

Another hugely distinctive feature of *Under A Watchful Eye* is the use of titles for each of the thirty one chapters of which the novel is composed. The titles are, well, "odd" – apparently random phrases which have little or no bearing on the contents of the chapters above which they are listed; *A Sack With a Narrow Opening*, *Carry Me Softly on Shoeless Feet* to name but two. What is revealed late on in the book is that these titles *do* have a significance, are in fact drawn from the writings of M L Hazzard himself, adding another layer of self-referential metafiction to the mix.

The novel is in three parts, all of which are given titles too, the first of which, *Yellow Teeth*, directly references the short story in which the Ewan character first appeared. (The other two are *This Prison of the Flesh* and *Through the Mist*). Some of Adam's other novels are divided into parts too and – much like the names he chooses for his characters – there's some enjoyment to be had in deriving the origins of them.

---

[98] A particular favourite of mine, second person, makes fleeting appearances throughout the novels, most commonly when describing the events of characters' dreams.

The first novel to be divided into parts was *The Ritual*, two in fact, reflecting the switch from visceral to psychological horror described earlier. The choice of titles is a clever one, the names reflecting both the narratives they contain and at the same time referencing heavy metal music, a sub-category of which, Black Metal, provides the ethos and motivation for the members of Blood Frenzy.

Part One is titled *Beneath the Remains* – a direct reference to the horrors lurking beneath the abandoned church the hikers stumble upon but also the title of the third album by Sepultura. Part Two is *South of Heaven* – somewhere Luke finds himself very far from and also the title of Slayer's fourth album.

The follow up novel, *Last Days*, is also divided into parts. In addition, individual chapters are given dates and locations, much as films do – especially of the made-for-TV variety – when scenes change, something entirely in keeping with the cinematic subject nature of the book[99].

Part One is called *The Process* which, following on from the music-related template established in *The Ritual* could have referred to the fifth album from American metal band Skinny Puppy but is much more likely to refer to the Process Church of the Final Judgement, a group of Scientologists-cum-Satanists from the 60s and 70s based in London, Mexico and the USA who had links to the Manson Family. Undoubtedly the inspiration for the Temple of the Last Days.

Part Two is *Helter Skelter*, originally a song by The Beatles but one which gained notoriety after Charles Manson used it as a name for his version of the race war he predicted was imminent, and used as motivation for the murders his "family" committed.

---

[99] In another, slightly meta touch a la *Under A Watchful Eye*, the parts are given epigraphs using quotes from the fictional Irvine Levine's book which is also called *Last Days*.

Part Three is *White Night*, a reference to Jim Jones who used the term to describe meetings with his cult in Jonestown in which options for escaping from the CIA were discussed. Among the options were mass suicide.

Part Four needs no detective work, *The Temple of the Last Days* referring directly to the cult which features in the novel itself.

Subdivision into parts is eschewed by the next book, *House of Small Shadows* but then reintroduced for *No One Gets Out Alive*. Part One, *Closer By Darkness Than Light*, is further subdivided into Day One, Day Two etc (all the way to Day Nine), something that put me very much in mind of the subtitle inserts in Kubrick's film version of *The Shining*. Part Two references this, (the total number of days in which Steph was trapped in 2 Edgehill Rd), called as it is *Nine Days in Hell*[100].

Other than *Under A Watchful Eye*, the only other novel divided into parts is *The Reddening*. This time the choice is for nice, straightforward (and short) titles which have archaeological connotations but also nicely fit into a classic three act structure; *Origins*, *Excavations* and *Relics* – setting up back story and context, acting to resolve the problems which arise as a result of the first act (excavating the truth behind what is happening around Divilmouth) then resolution and aftermath, the narrative now become history.

Prologues feature in all but four of the novels, named as such in *Apartment 16*, *The Ritual* and *Last Days* whilst the opening chapters of *Banquet For The Damned*, *House of Small Shadows* and *The Reddening* (in this case more than one chapter) serve the same purpose of setting up the narrative to come. In *Cunning Folk*, the prologue has its

---

[100] Which would have made a fine title for Steph's own book about her experiences. Instead, she goes with the snappier *No One Gets Out Alive*.

own title: *Before the Beginning* and, given that the novel is adapted from a screenplay, can be regarded as a pre-title sequence.

Whereas prologues are typically set in the past with regards the events of the novel itself, that of *The Ritual*, and the opening chapter of *House of Small Shadows* are set at times after the beginning of the stories, offering up glimpses of what is to come.

In effect, they're not prologues at all, but the beginnings of the narrative proper which are then followed by flashbacks. In *House of Small Shadows*, it's Catherine's arrival at the Red House which opens the book, the narrative then going back in time to a week earlier when the commission for the work she is to undertake is arranged.

The time difference is much smaller in *The Ritual*, with the events of the "prologue" occurring only four hours ahead of the flashback. This allows for a wonderful opening scene which whets the appetite straight from the off, and the opening paragraph of the book, in my opinion, ranks among the finest horror literature has to offer:

And on the second day things did not get better. The rain fell hard and cold, the white sun never broke through the low grey cloud, and they were lost. But it was the dead thing they found hanging from a tree that changed the trip beyond recognition. All four of them saw it at the same time.

This technique of presenting action then jumping back in time and following the narrative back to the starting point is one that's used as a framing device within the texts of other of Adam's novels.

Lost Girl features a number of scenes which "start at the end" before flashing back. In fact most of the Father's encounters with the paedophiles he "interrogates" are described in this fashion, the scenes beginning with his return to whichever hotel room he is staying in at that point then describing his recollections of the events which preceded.

Notable examples of this technique occur in *The Reddening* too. The ritual sacrifice of Steve is presented via Kat's memories of what happened rather than in real time; the rampage of Creel towards the book's climax is described in retrospect after its aftermath has been vividly described[101] - the chapter which describes it subtitled "*a few minutes earlier.*"

Gracey's trip to hospital following her horrific accident in *Cunning Folk* is also presented in flashback, described through the recollections of Tom and acting as a catalyst to spur him into ever more extreme measures to combat the threat of the Moots.

Only two of the novels feature epilogues (although some do have extended sequences set after the main events of the narrative are completed). In *Apartment 16* the final chapter acts as an epilogue, focusing on Stephen, the head porter rather than either of the book's protagonists Seth and Apryl. This is then followed by the epilogue itself which features Seth's landlord examining the room he has vacated. This is really supplementary to the plot as a whole but the chapter with Stephen which precedes it is hugely important, relaying the message that the menace which haunted the corridors of Barrington House is not gone, that the evil persists.

This is the same message the epilogue of *No One Gets Out Alive* conveys. Despite her successes in escaping

---

[101] A possible proto-dereliction.

from the clutches of Black Maggie, not once but twice, Steph/Amber is all too aware that she can never let her defences down; the battles may be won but the war goes on.

Chapter Six

The Nevillesque

I began my re-read of Adam's novels in February of 2022 with *Apartment 16* and worked my way through the books in subsequent publication order until finishing with *Banquet For The Damned* in June. An advance copy of *The Vessel* arrived a couple of months later, making it the only one of the novels to have had a single readthrough only. The reasoning behind leaving his debut novel until last was to allow a more detailed analysis of the book with respect to the themes and motifs which characterise his writing; this would be where they originated, this would be the birthplace of the Nevillesque.

And so it proved. Coming to the novel again after having read and re-read the others allowed the identification of many of the key elements that make Adam's books what they are; the incredible atmosphere his writing generates, the disturbing imagery he creates, "ordinary" people thrust into the world of the supernatural.

It's an incredibly accomplished first novel with assured and confident writing throughout. Here is a writer with a distinctive vision and the skills to convey it to readers. It's also a novel that wears its influences on its sleeve and possibly the closest to a recreation of the classic ghost stories that provided much of the inspiration for Adam's own writing. The motif of a person awakening to find a figure in the room appears here a number of times, undoubtedly a nod to the conclusion of M R James' story *Oh, Whistle, and I'll Come to You, My Lad* which features the same scenario. It's an experience shared by Apryl in

Apartment 16, Catherine in *House of Small Shadows*, Steph (most significantly of all) in *No One Gets Out Alive*, Seb in *Under A Watchful Eye* and Jess in *The Vessel*.

James is also the author of the story *A Thin Ghost*, a description which perfectly fits the spectral figures which haunt the pages of Adam's novels and must surely have been an influence whilst the device of using artefacts as a beacon for supernatural forces he employed in *Casting the Runes* has echoes in *Last Days*, *No One Gets Out Alive* and *Cunning Folk*.

References and homages to other authors from that golden age are scattered throughout the novels – the scene in which Gracey stumbles upon the woodland glade in *Cunning Folk* is, to my mind, very reminiscent of the denouement to Machen's *The White People* – but the author with whom Adam shares the greatest similarity in terms of tone is possibly Algernon Blackwood whose weird tales inspire feelings as much of awe as terror, that awe often generated by the natural world settings he employed in many of his stories.

Those similarities are most overt between Blackwood's novella *The Wendigo* and *The Ritual*, both of which feature ancient monsters in forests. Whilst the titular beast of Blackwood's story is an established part of Native American tradition, Moder is an original creation, as are the other monsters which populate Adam's novels; The Blood Friends, Black Maggie, Old Creel and The Sow Beneath the Earth. And yet all of them feel as if they are "real" beasts of myth and legend – indeed, the first time I read *No One Gets Out Alive* I actually tried to do some research on Black Maggie before reviewing the book, so convinced was I that the folklore around her was genuine.

Of all the monsters he has created, the Blood Friends of *Last Days* come closest to showing "traditional" characteristics of horror story creatures with their aversion to light and salt – references to both vampires and demons. As the thrilling conclusion to the book shows they can be killed too, something that remains in doubt about the other Nevill monsters. Immortal, and therefore worshipped as gods, these other monsters embody a running theme in Adam's novels, that of the persistence of ancient evil. Whilst the protagonists of the novels may survive their encounters with these creatures they do not defeat them; the monsters remain, and will continue to do so despite the best efforts of weak humanity. From the perspective of the monsters these are little more than fleeting interactions.

Another recurring theme in the novels is that of death – and what happens after. These thanatological concerns make an appearance in *Apartment 16* in which it is posited that, as well as allowing a glimpse into the Vortex, the actual moment of death reveals the "other" incarnation of the beholder, the alternate identity of all of us which exists within the maelstrom of that other dimension, a notion similar to that expressed in Machen's *The White People*; the half of the soul that is madness.

In *Under A Watchful Eye,* mention is made of the "hinderers in the passage", (the name providing the title for chapter 10 of the book), discarnate entities who prevent the souls of dead (or in this case astrally projecting) people from returning to their bodies. These hinderers bear similarities to the "patrons" who appear in the philosophy of the Kings in *Lost Girl*. However, rather than impeding and blocking the souls of the departed, they are more akin to guardian angels, aiding and guiding new inhabitants of the "afterdeath".

The "classic" voice Adam adopted for his debut novel has remained in place throughout all the subsequent books and is even to be found in the most recent, The Vessel, despite its origins as a screenplay. Witness the opening paragraph:

> *A stillness profound enough to be uncanny hushes a woodland glade. Trees encircle the placid water of a circular pond therein, the surface a black mirror reflecting a sombre sky.*

Given the book's cinematic origins this can be regarded as an establishing shot, setting the scene (literally) for the action to come. It's little surprise that Adam has turned his hand to writing screenplays as his novels have all been hugely cinematic. Whilst there are those who might be sniffy at such a thought I regard it as evidence of great skill as a writer. To be able to create atmosphere, and describe images so clearly that they arrive in readers' heads fully formed is the mark of fine writing indeed. And yes, the novels are plot driven – again, something that is regarded by some as a lesser form of writing but those plots are anchored by brilliantly drawn characters and, of course, enhanced by their poetic prose[102].

At no point do the plots ever feel contrived; the flow of action and the characters' reactions to events are all entirely authentic. Yes, there are set-pieces – in keeping with the cinematic feel of the books – but none feel shoe-horned in with the plot having to alter to accommodate them, rather adding to and enhancing the narrative, are natural progressions of the story.

---

[102] An oxymoron I will defend to my dying breath.

Working on this book has been a hugely enjoyable experience. In recent years I've discovered that there is a particular joy in revisiting books already read; it's a different kind of joy to that when experiencing a book for the first time, uncovering its secrets and allowing the author to take you to new and exciting places but a joy nonetheless. The difference between the excitement and thrill of new love and the comfort of a well-established relationship if you will.

Aside from *Banquet For The Damned*, I read the books in publication order, the better to observe the evolution and development of ideas, influences and style. In every case I believe that I enjoyed the re-reads more than my first encounters with the novels. As with watching films, familiarity with the stories allows for more attention to the fine detail on repeated viewings, the nuances and subtleties that may get lost on the headlong rush to find out what happens next that occurs on first exposure.

As debut novels go, *Banquet For The Damned* is hugely impressive, ranking alongside the best of them and, much as Barker's *The Damnation Game* did, provides a perfect showcase for the style and technique of a very distinctive voice in horror fiction. It wasn't the first of Adam's novels that I read – I had to hunt it down on second hand sites as it was out of print when I got round to it – but I'm certain that I would have been immediately hooked on his writing had I read it when it was first released. It's a book that's brimming with ideas, maybe too many – a history of the coven and its origins in Hungary along with links to Polish Upyrs (vampires) is covered in a few paragraphs despite its potential for expansion – but some definitely provide the foundations for the horrors to come in later novels.

As the spreadsheets and reams of scribbled notes I produced over the course of writing this book will testify, *Apartment 16* is one of the books to have the fewest links to the Nevillesque but this does little to diminish its stature as a brilliant work of horror fiction in its own right. Indeed, a whole book could be dedicated to it alone, such are the themes and symbolism lurking within its pages and the corridors of Barrington House; the duality of the real world and the Vortex reflected (literally as well as metaphorically) in the use of twin protagonists, the notion of "other" incarnations of personality, the extensive use of mirrors and the imagery they allow throughout.

I think *The Ritual* is the book where Adam properly hit his stride. It ranks highly in my personal ratings of his work because so much of its subject matter appealed to me. It was monsters that first sparked my interest in the horror genre and so it was hugely gratifying to find a novel employing one to such brilliant effect.

One thing I noticed on re-read was how awful Dom and Phil are. It's possibly down to the fact that I'd watched the film version of the novel a couple of times before the re-read; the cinematic versions of these characters are still pretty annoying but nowhere near as horrible as the originals in the book. The important thing of course is that these aren't cardboard cut-out bad guys, their views and utterances may be reprehensible, bordering on toxic, but are a manifestation of their expertly drawn characters. Far from rejoicing in their misogyny, the novel shows it as a flaw, a weakness, and is actually an indictment of a certain way of male behaviour.

Whilst *The Ritual* ranks highly in my personal list, the top spot goes to the follow-up novel *Last Days*. The monster lover in me rejoiced at the Blood Friends which I regard as Adam's most terrifying creations. Much has been made already of two scenes in particular to be found in this book but the emotions they engendered in me on re-read were as profound as the first time I encountered them. The description of the triptych is one of the most atmospheric sequences I've ever read, the transformation of visual imagery into written word without equal. The reader gets to see exactly what Kyle is seeing, shares with him the feelings of dread the images evoke. And as for the "found footage" scene… Brilliantly constructed, (and hugely cinematic), the first time I read it I literally had to put the book down to compose myself. Knowing what was to come on my second read I could "enjoy" the scene a lot more and was able to appreciate just how cleverly written it was. Perfect.

House of Small Shadows is Adam's most gothic novel, wonderfully creating a sense of the past; one can almost smell the old leather of the chairs in the Red House (as well as the formaldehyde and other taxidermy chemicals). Imagery is the key here, the displays of anthropomorphic taxidermy creating a sinister atmosphere which transcends plain weirdness. Of all the novels, it's the one to which the term "creepy" is most appropriately applied, a disorientating, haunting quality permeating its pages which makes the violence and gore which features in its conclusion all the more striking.

There's a continuity of sorts with the next novel which also features a young, single woman trapped in a building against her will but whereas I could picture *House of Small Shadows* as a Merchant Ivory production[103], *No One Gets Out Alive* is definitely Ken Loach territory.[104]

It's a tough read, one that was no easier second time round, and one that requires stamina being the longest of

---

[103] If a). they made horror films and b). they were both still alive.

[104] If a). he made horror films and b). the film hadn't already been made by Santiago Menghini.

Adam's novels. It's quite an achievement that the tension he creates from the get-go is maintained throughout, even managing to intensify as the narrative progresses. Whereas there was an element of frustration at Catherine's seeming inability to remove herself from the Red House here it's sympathy which is evoked at Steph's plight as her choices, and chances of escape are whittled away one by one.

On my first read I felt the transition into the mythology of Black Maggie felt a little abrupt but this was definitely a result of ignoring the finer details in a rush to see what happens next. My re-read helped to identify the subtle clues left along the way to set up the supernatural elements alongside the human horrors.

And what horrors they are! Fergal and Knacker are truly awful men with no depravity too low for them to descend to. Both characters could easily have fitted into the next novel *Lost Girl*, taking their place in the array of lowlifes and paedophiles the Father encounters on his search for his missing daughter.

Reading these two books back to back as I did was a gruelling experience; plumbing the depths of human behaviour for such an extended period of time is not something I would recommend. Which, of course, is in its own way a compliment to the strength of the writing in these two novels, managing to create such horribly realistic characters that to spend time with them is such a negative experience.

Lost Girl is possibly the least Nevillesque of the novels, its horrors arising from human rather than supernatural origins. It's basically a revenge thriller, a description the generic cover design of a silhouetted figure pasted onto a background certainly reinforces. It's very much a departure from what Adam had produced thus far and, I have to admit, the first time I read it the thought crossed my mind that his publishers may have encouraged him to write something more "mainstream".

In retrospect I can see how silly a notion that was. Indeed, this may be the most personal book Adam has written, encapsulating his own fears – for the environmental crisis and harm against his own daughter – and creating a narrative in which he could express them both, perhaps vicariously examining his own limits as to how far he would himself go to protect his family.

And then there's *Under A Watchful Eye*, a return to supernatural horror but also evidence of an author willing to experiment with the process of writing itself. It's the only one of his novels to feature a "twist", a reveal that alters the whole nature of the reading experience and which casts new light on all that has gone before. And it works brilliantly.

The novel marks a turning point too. After *Under A Watchful Eye*, publication of all of Adam's books was undertaken by his own press Ritual Limited. One of the reasons for this shift was to allow himself full creative control over the product, freedom to do what he wanted with his fiction, something I believe he was initiating with the metafictional delights of *Under A Watchful Eye*.

It's a decision I can only applaud given that the first novel produced by Ritual Limited was the epic *The Reddening*. To reiterate, in my opinion this is the quintessential Nevill novel, the ultimate embodiment of the Nevillesque. As touched on in the Profondo Rosso section I believe that this novel had probably been taking up space in Adam's subconscious for many years, an accumulation of all the images and ideas his writing had created. This is the book that says "this is what I do", and therefore it's no surprise that he wanted full control over how it was presented to the world.

The experimentation with the form being his own master allowed resulted in the next two novels, *Cunning Folk* and *The Vessel*, both of which were adapted from his own screenplays. Both continue the folk horror theme cemented in *The Reddening* (but prevalent throughout all the previous books) and it seems that that is the sub-genre Adam feels most comfortable in.

This willingness, eagerness even, to try new ways of expressing ideas is hugely gratifying to see as a reader and I look forward greatly to whatever emerges next from one of the most creative imaginations in the horror genre. Whilst some things may change and evolve, it's reassuring to know that some things will stay the same; whichever direction Adam chooses to take going forward, one thing is certain – the signature moves and peculiarities that already mark him out as a distinctive and recognisable literary voice will travel with him. The Nevillesque, like the Red, will abide.

ACKNOWLEDGEMENTS

Huge thanks to my wife Judith for her support and encouragement during the writing of this book and for taking the time out to read through the third, or possibly fourth, draft to offer comments and suggestions. Even though she married me, horror really isn't her thing which makes the help she's given me even more special.

Thanks too to Neil Williams for the wonderful imagery that graces the cover of this book; his skill and creativity never fail to impress me and he's done another incredible job here.

And thanks, of course, to Adam himself for writing the books which inspired me in the first place as well as the interest he has shown in this project since its inception and the advice and encouragement he has offered along the way.

Printed in Poland
by Amazon Fulfillment
Poland Sp. z o.o., Wrocław
10 March 2023

7159c230-9799-4cfc-92f8-3937c68c9b96R01